Pub Walks
on
Exmoor

Philip Pond

Published by Sigma Leisure – an imprint of
Sigma Press, 1 South Oak Lane, Wilmslow, Cheshire SK9 6AR, England.

British Library Cataloguing in Publication Data
A CIP record for this book is available from the British Library.

ISBN: 1-85058-308-0

Typesetting and Design by: Sigma Press, Wilmslow, Cheshire.

Maps by: Manchester Free Press

Text photographs: Philip Pond

Cover photograph: The Royal Oak, Winsford, arguably the prettiest pub on Exmoor

Printed and Bound by
Manchester Free Press, Unit E3, Longford Trading Estate, Thomas Street, Stretford, Manchester M32 0JT. Telephone 061 864 4540

General Disclaimer

Whilst every effort has been made to ensure that the information given in this book is correct, neither the publisher nor the author accept any responsibility for any inaccuracy.

By Way Of Introduction

When I set out to write this book, it was in the belief that I already knew Exmoor. Here I am writing this one year, tens of pubs, dozens of walks and countless miles later. And I realise now just how little I knew then, how much I have learnt in the intervening months and what a vast amount there is still to know about Somerset's and Devon's shared national park.

The more I discover about Exmoor, the more I want to know. The park is that sort of place. It whets the appetite, and not just for an intimate knowledge of its past and present but intimately to experience the moor in all its moods. Mind you, having walked and written this book over the course of a year, I have already witnessed spring, summer, autumn and, an albeit mild, winter on Exmoor.

I know for a fact too that walking is the best way of experiencing Exmoor at its most intimate. There is no better way of getting close to the soul of this national park, or any other come to that.

I would not have been able to write this book and achieve what I have achieved without the help of several individuals and organisations. I would like to thank in particular Wendy Fellingham and her colleagues at the Ordnance Survey (what would I have done without those Pathfinder maps!); Warren Davis and his colleagues at the National Trust (the service and facilities the NT provide are second to none) and Kathleen and Victor Hornsby and their children, Joseph and Vickie, who put up so uncomplainingly with my comings and goings. Special thanks to my own children, Julie, Phillip, Andrew and Sarah, for being guinea pigs in testing out these walks.

Most importantly of all, my biggest 'thank you' must go to my wife, Mary: without her help, support, encouragement, patience and for-bearance (in other words her love), I never would have got the book done, in or out of time.

Philip Pond

CONTENTS

BACKGROUND

THE WALKS AND THE PUBS

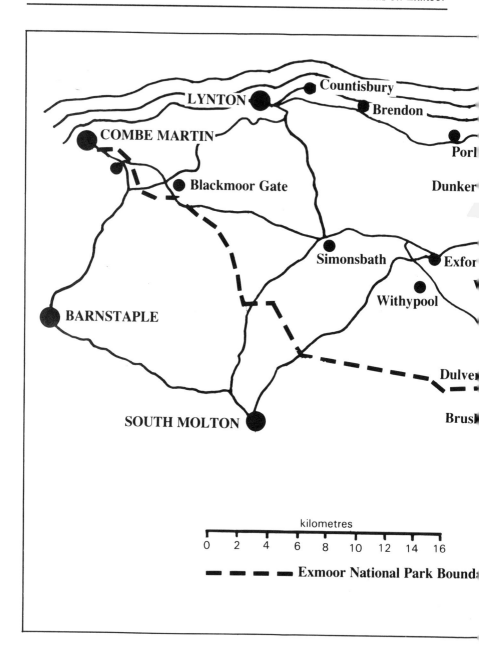

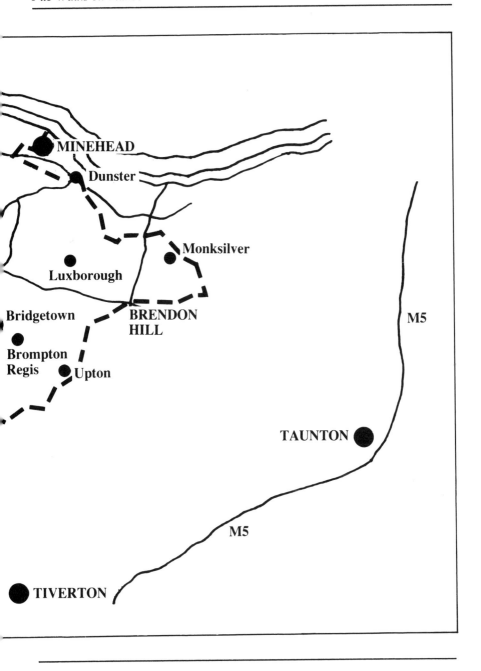

Exmoor offers a wide choice of walks – this signpost indicates the pleasures and perils around Monksilver (Walk 10)

How Exmoor Offers Extra

Red deer, Lorna Doone, cream teas, cider: those are the images most likely to spring to mind at the mention of Exmoor. And in many ways they accurately sum up much of what this national park is all about.

The red deer, standing 4ft high at the shoulder and weighing 20 stone, is Britain's largest wild land animal. A romantic novel rather than a piece of history, R. D. Blackmore's 'Lorna Doone' is the supreme legend of Exmoor but nonetheless based in fact. Cream teas have become synonymous with holidays and leisure time in the West Country as a whole. And cider? Well it cannot be coincidence, surely, that more of it comes up from Somerset seemingly than any other part of Britain.

It goes without saying that there is much, much more to Exmoor than deer, Doones and diets. The difficulty is knowing where to begin.

Its starting point in the form in which we know it today is perhaps the best beginning. Located mainly in Somerset but with a small section in Devon, the moor was designated a national park four decades ago in 1954 and, at 686sq km (265sq miles), ranks as the second smallest. A few statistics will set the scene.

Population is only around 10,000. They are mainly concentrated in five small towns, four on or near the coast and all on the edges of the moor. Likewise, the only major roads skirt the interior, sticking to the coastline in the north and bisecting the tips of the park to east and west. The seaside resort of Minehead, just outside the boundary to the north east, is the largest centre of population.

Dotted around within the park are scattered a much larger number of small villages, attractive and rewarding for the visitor. They tend to be concentrated in the often deep and wooded valleys, the combes which are such a characteristic feature of Exmoor. That is where the roads and rivers run too, reflecting the upland nature of the moor as a whole. An exception is the more gently rolling area formed by the Brendon Hills in the east.

The 29-mile-long coastline is the highest in England, sometimes over 300m (1,000ft), with spectacular cliffs which in places drop 244m (800ft) sheer into the sea. That is the Bristol Channel – next stop, South Wales. The Welsh coastline is clearly visible from several points on the moor, even well inland.

The coastline apart, Exmoor is not an area of extremes. Here you have a gentler, kinder landscape than its near neighbour, Dartmoor, to the south. A high proportion of the moor lies more than 300m (1,000ft) above sea level but this is a plateau and only in isolated spots does it break the 500m barrier. Dunkery Beacon, at 519m, clearly counts as the high point.

The Romans seem to have found the environment here not at all to their liking. But there is no shortage of Bronze Age and Iron Age burial mounds and stone circles to be found. None is spectacular but more than 2,000 sites or groupings was the estimated total according to one survey.

Despite 'Exmoor Forest' appearing on the map and all those wooded combes, you will not find vast stretches of tree-covered upland within this national park. The term, which dates back to Anglo Saxon times, relates to Exmoor's popularity and role as a royal hunting ground in medieval times. In fact, only about a tenth of the land area is given over to commercial forestry and deciduous woodland combined.

Rather more than half has been enclosed as farmland, farmed the traditional way. As a result, Exmoor has been described as the British countryside at its best, criss-crossed, where cultivated, with hedges, trees and walls and no great prairie spreads or ranches. You can expect to find plenty of beech hedges and stone and slate boundary walls here.

The rest of the land, well over a quarter, is open country. Much of that last is heather moorland, one of the main reasons for Exmoor's appeal. It appears at its most attractive in late summer when the moors are covered in a blanket of deep purple blooms.

The best way to see those and everything else Exmoor has to offer, of course, is by walking. You will find 600 miles of public rights of way to help you on your way. The activities of the National Trust, which owns a tenth of the national park, are a bonus in terms of access for ramblers.

The 18th century poets William Wordsworth and Samuel Coleridge were both keen walkers in the area. It could be that when he wrote 'Kubla Khan' in a farmhouse near Porlock on the northern edge of the park, Coleridge had the deep, tree-lined combes of Exmoor in mind. Consider his words:

'*And here were forests ancient as the hills*
Enfolding sunny spots of greenery.
But O that deep romantic chasm which slanted
Down the green hill athwart a cedarn cover!
A savage place!'

Whether he did or not, the combination of wooded streams, heather covered moors and tall, plunging cliffs is a magnetic one. There are other images too which will stay in the mind's eye long after walking on Exmoor:

The ponies, with their long, hairy overcoats, which are not truly wild but are allowed to run free.

The local terms, with their rich imagery: ball, for hill; linney, for a farm building; lynchet, a terrace; shippon, a cowshed; urts, for whortleberries; vuzz, gorse; bizgy, a mattock (an agricultural tool).

The place names too, which conjure up such vivid and colourful images: Badgworthy Water, Pinkery Pond, The Chains, Great Hangman, Devil's Cheesewring, Larkbarrow, Hoaroak Water, Blackmoor, Withycombe, Hawkcombe Head, Withiel Florey, Watersmeet, Timberscombe . . .

Pure poetry.

Which is perhaps an appropriate point to return to Coleridge. . .

'The light has left the summit of the hill,
Though still a sunny gleam lies beautiful,
Aslant the ivied beacon. Now farewell,
Farewell, awhile, O soft and silent spot!
On the green sheep-track, up the heathy hill
Homeward I wend my way; and lo! Recalled
From bodings that have well-nigh wearied me,
I find myself upon the brow, and pause
Startled! And after lonely sojourning
In such a quiet and surrounding nook,
This burst of prospect, here the shadowy main,
Dim-tinted, there the mighty majesty
Of that huge amphitheatre of rich
And elmy fields. . . '

How To Get There

By Road

From London and the South-East the M4 motorway is the most popular route. From the M4 join the M5 at Junction 20 near Bristol and, turning south, follow the motorway to Bridgwater (Junction 23) or Taunton (Junction 25) or Junction 27 and follow the North Devon Link Road to Bolham. Northern areas of Exmoor can then be reached via the A39 or A358 and southern parts via the A361/North Devon Link. A quieter route from the South East is by way of the M3, A303 and A358.

From the Midlands it is the M5 all the way until you reach Junctions 23, 25 or 27. From those, follow the directions above.

Long distance coach services operate to Taunton, Minehead and Barnstaple from most regional centres. Enquire locally.

By Rail

There are fast inter-city services to Taunton and beyond to Exeter. For western parts of Exmoor change at Exeter for the branch line to Barnstaple. From these stations it is necessary to transfer to the bus services for destinations within the national park. The West Somerset Railway provides a Taunton – Minehead – Taunton service (bus link between Taunton and Bishops Lydeard). Telephone Minehead (0643) 704996 (General Enquiries) or 0643 707650 (Talking Timetable) for further details.

Local Public Transport

An Exmoor public transport timetable is obtainable from information centres, libraries and sub post offices.

Services linking Exmoor with Lynton, Barnstaple, Bampton, Tiverton and other places in Devon are operated by various bus companies. Full details are available from Devon County Council's bus enquiry line (0392 382800).

Southern National Coach Station, Tower Street, Taunton (tel: 0823 272033) operates services between Taunton and Minehead.

Scarlet Coaches, 53 The Avenue, Minehead, (tel: 0643 704204) operates services as follows: Minehead – Dulverton – Tiverton; Minehead – Porlock – Lynmouth; Minehead – Porlock Weir.

Kingdom's Tours Ltd, Westfield, Exeter Road, Tiverton (tel: 0884 252373) runs services from Tiverton to Dulverton.

The following also operate services in the area:

W. Ridler & Son, Jury Road, Dulverton (tel: 0398 23398).

D. F. Stevens, The Garage, Withycombe, Minehead (tel: 0984 40246).

Red Bus, North Devon Ltd, Coney Avenue, Barnstaple (tel: 0271 45444.)

The Lyn Valley Bus Service, using minibuses, operates year-round to destinations in Devon and Somerset, daily in season, including the Doone Country (tel: 0598 53320/52470).

The Walks

There are 25 walks in this guide and they offer nothing if not variety. Choosing these two dozen plus one was not easy. You could do 250 walks on Exmoor and still not cover all the ground or see all that there is to see and enjoy within this national park. So the choice of which ones to include and which ones to leave out had to be largely subjective.

So how did I choose them? All sorts of factors came into consideration. But basically I opted for routes which were scenically attractive, not too demanding, short enough to cover in no more than half a day and near a good pub. (My definition of an agreeable ale-house is set out on another page.)

One thing is for certain: every one of the 25 offers something special for the walker.

To be more specific, you can expect the following in these pages . . .

Distance: the shortest is less than two miles, the longest nearly ten. But nearly every route offers options: short-cuts, detours, extensions. Which means that you could if you wished turn some of these routes into much longer rambles. Alternatively several can be shortened should you decide part way round that you have had enough or do not wish to cover the whole distance in one go.

Time: the speed at which ramblers walk varies. If you assume half an hour per mile, you won't be far out. Distances are given for all of the rambles so it is easy to work out the approximate amount of time needed for each. On several of these routes there is much that you could see and do if you wished: ruins to explore, a picnic spot to enjoy, views to savour, a beach to comb, hills to climb, a dam to investigate, old monuments and relics to examine, even the odd stately home or castle to visit if the fancy takes you. And that's not allowing for bird-watching, stalking wildlife or nature study.

Shape: every single one of these walks is circular. Personally, I dislike linear routes: why cover the same ground twice if you can cover new ground on the return leg? Almost inevitably, however, there are cases where the initial leg is common but in no case does this extend to any more than a small proportion of the overall distance covered.

Severity: there are no extremes within these walks, no precipitous climbs or hair-raising descents. Some of them involve fairly steep hills but those are the exception rather than the rule. And in any case, what is a coast or country ramble without a bit of effort? Exerting yourself is part of the pleasure.

Surfaces: rambles mainly follow footpaths, bridleways and green lanes. But, inevitably, in order to construct circular walks it has sometimes been necessary to include stretches along lanes (of the quiet, country sort) and, in a very few cases, roads. However, nowhere on these metalled sections is the volume of traffic going to comprise anything more than the occasional car.

Access: the vast majority of these routes are based on public rights of way. Some are supplemented by permissive paths. So, for example, on the Countisbury walks, there are stretches over land owned by the National Trust. They are not rights of way but the public are allowed and encouraged to use them. Nowhere on any of these routes do you trespass.

Obstructions: the nature of the countryside and the system of land ownership in this country can on occasion result in footpaths becoming overgrown with the passage of time. You may come across stiles which are blocked and gates which are locked. Unaccompanied bulls in fields crossed by rights of way are not unknown (although I did not come across a single instance on any of these walks). Where you physically cannot follow a public footpath because of such obstructions, you are entitled by law to make a detour to get round them, even if that involves trespassing. But if it comes to that, be considerate of the landowner and make your detour as short as possible.

Signs: you will find signposts or waymarks along every single one of these rambles. That does not mean every hundred yards, nor even at regular albeit infrequent intervals. Waymarking and signposting are, to say the least, haphazard on Exmoor although this national park is probably better served than most. For example, at one extreme, routes which cross National Trust property are particularly well served;

whereas those outside the fringes of the national park were, not surprisingly, almost devoid of indicators. Still, finding your way is part of the challenge and produces a lot of satisfaction. Which brings me to:

Maps: I used Ordnance Survey Pathfinder maps throughout, and excellent and invaluable they are too. But first the bad news. Annoyingly when I walked these parts, despite Exmoor being a national park it was necessary to have no fewer than seven separate sheets to cover the complete area. (The numbers of the Pathfinders are given in the relevant chapters.) The good news, at time of writing, is that the Ordnance Survey are shortly due to publish one of their value-for-money Outdoor Leisure Maps covering Exmoor. Which means that you should be able to buy just that one sheet to walk the whole of this national park. Not only will it cover the complete area at the same scale as the Pathfinders (1:25,000 or $2^1/_2$in to the mile) but you will get a lot of additional information shown as well. And, I hasten to add, at considerably less cost than buying seven separate sheets. You should be so lucky. As always, it pays to use a plastic map case to protect your investment. The rain and wind can destroy even a brand new map infuriatingly quickly, even without your folding and unfolding it every now and then.

Compass: not an essential but I would strongly recommend one. Exmoor, unlike Dartmoor, is a generally hospitable place and you cannot wander far without coming across signposts and waymarks, if not a lane, a road or human habitation. Nonetheless, there are still hairy areas out on the moorland and the weather can deteriorate most unpleasantly, especially during the winter months. Take my advice and carry both map and compass.

Clothing: don't underestimate the wind and rain. When you walk dictates the type of clothing you wear. But even during the summer months, it can be cold, wet and windy out on the moors. So go prepared, with waterproofs in a rucksack plus a jumper or fleece just in case. That way, you can almost guarantee the weather will be kind. (Leave them behind of course and the opposite will be true.)

Footwear: no-one is going to force you to wear anything other than what you prefer. Trainers are comfortable and widely worn. On a warm, sunny summer's day in the middle of a drought they would probably suffice on most if not all of these walks. But who can be certain in this country that it will not rain at any given time? So do yourself a favour and wear either walking shoes or, better still, boots. I used fabric boots which are tough yet lightweight. I also, as a general rule, wore gaiters with them too. On the occasions when I didn't, I regretted it. Even after all these years, I am still surprised at how muddy and messy one's legs get even on short walks over good surfaces. Gaiters are to be recommended.

Daysac: there will always be odds and ends which come in handy en route: binoculars, a drink, some sandwiches, sweets or chocolate, fruit, a jumper or fleece, a cagoule, spare film, a camera, the car keys, you name it. . . Carrying them in your pockets, slung around your neck or dangling over your shoulder is possible but usually not comfortable. A daysac makes more sense. Buy one of around 20-30 litres' capacity: you will find it a godsend, and not just for country rambles either.

Dogs: take the dog by all means but remember that when crossing fields containing livestock or passing through a farmyard, you must be sure to keep him/her under control. Don't forget: the law says that farmers have a right to shoot dogs which attack or even just chase their livestock. Should you take your pet, bear that in mind when deciding whether or not to use a lead.

Pubs: Immediately following are details of my choice of hostelries. Suffice to say here that each and every walk includes at least one inn at the beginning or en route. Some have two or more.

The Pubs

What makes a good pub? Asking the question is easy enough but answering it isn't. In fact there are probably as many answers as there are pubs. Large, small, old, modern, quiet, noisy, crowded, uncrowded: those are the sort of features people look for in their favourite hostelry (fortunately not all at the same time and in the same establishment). Then there is entertainment: live, canned, family, adult, traditional, electronic, non-existent, non-stop. Don't forget either the facilities: family room, no smoking area, restaurant, public bar, saloon. Nor have I mentioned the standard of service provided, the type of clientele and prices. All are factors which play a part in your choice of local.

Arguably most important of all, however, is what you drink.

Which brings me to the basis for the selection of pubs in this guide. The choice is mine. But perhaps I ought to say 'ours'. Because I was very much guided in my selection by the views of the Somerset branch of CAMRA.

This branch of the Campaign for Real Ale is an active, committed and enthusiastic one. So much so that its members have in the past produced their own good pub guide. They have a declared interest in good beer. And by definition they are intimately familiar with the area, its hostelries, its breweries, its publicans, its landlords, every aspect of the public house in this part of the country.

Now you may or may not be a lover of real ale. You may prefer keg or bottled or lager or cider or soft drinks or spirits or whatever, and good luck to you. But in a sense that is irrelevant. Because in my experience if a tavern serves real ale, whether direct from the cask or by handpump, it means at the very least greater choice for the drinker. The kegs and bottles and ciders and so on are still on offer. But you can choose to quaff real ale if you wish. Which can be no bad thing.

Strange but true, however, is that inns which serve real ale tend to be different. They are often more welcoming, more hospitable, more sensitive to the needs and wants of their customers, more inclined to provide the sort of service and the type of setting, not to mention atmosphere, which is conducive to a convivial evening (or lunchtime or whatever).

Don't get me wrong. I am not saying that is always the case: there will invariably be exceptions. But as a general rule, in my experience the real ale pub is a better pub.

A total of 25 feature in this guide. They vary enormously.

At one extreme are the likes of the Rockford Inn in Rockford and the Lowtrow Cross in Upton. They are small, cosy, unpretentious inns. Your typical village local.

Then there are the modest 'village locals' which although in a much larger centre of population offer much the same features and atmosphere. Examples are the Bridge in Dulverton and the Old Ship Aground in Minehead.

At the other extreme sizewise are the grand hotel and country club set, for instance the Luttrell Arms in Dunster, the Exmoor Forest in Simonsbath, the Royal Oak in Withypool and the Carnarvon Arms in Brushford. All fly fishing, game shooting and à la carte menus.

In between come the town taverns, generally of good size and offering a good range of services and facilities. Take for example the Dunster Castle in Dunster, The Ship in Porlock, Kildare Lodge in Minehead and The Lion in Dulverton.

A special mention, because they offered something a little bit special or out of the ordinary, for these ale-houses:

The George in Brompton Regis: it nearly didn't make it – the landlord will tell you why.

The Royal Oak, Porlock: caters particularly well for families with children of whatever age.

The Dunkery Beacon, Wootton Courtney: real ale straight from the cask.

The White Horse, Exford: one of the widest selections of real ale: five from which to choose the last time I visited.

The Crown: if you want to see the Devon & Somerset Staghounds on Boxing Day.

Ralegh's Cross, Brendon Hill: non-smokers as well as families with children are catered for here.

Notley Arms, Monksilver: the number of awards it has won in the good food and good pub guides says it all.

Exmoor Sandpiper, Countisbury: the bars just go on and on. And so does the list of names this inn has had.

Old Station House, Blackmoor Gate: facilities for families, and just look at that skittle alley.

Hunter's Inn, Heddon Valley: a name to conjure with and a setting to dream about.

The Royal Oak, Winsford: the prettiest pub and the prettiest village on Exmoor.

The Badgers Holt, Bridgetown: small is beautiful.

Last but far from being least, a real gem: the **Royal Oak** (yes, another) in Luxborough. Wherever else you quench your thirst on Exmoor, make sure to take your custom to the Blazing Stump as it is also known. Real olde worlde flavour, and genuine too. Really. It's all low ceilings, flagstones and scrubbed wooden furniture plus the best choice in real ale of any inn I visited on Exmoor. Pay them a visit.

What time?

Despite a change in the law allowing pubs in England to open for 12 hours a day on Mondays to Saturdays, few on Exmoor do. The vast majority (the Castle Hotel in Dunster was an exception) have stuck to the old opening times. Which usually means 11am or 12 noon till 2.30pm or 3pm and any time between 5pm and 7pm till 11pm. On Sundays the norm is noon till 3pm and 7pm till 11pm. But check in advance to be on the safe side, especially as 'time gentlemen please' can be called at different times in summer and winter.

Finally, it's be-kind-to-publicans-time. They want your custom and you want their services. What they don't want is your muddy boots spreading muck'n'bullets all over the bar. So be considerate, clean them off as best you can before entering and, if possible, leave your footwear just inside the door. Cheers!

Breweries and Beers

Visit the pubs mentioned in this guide and you will come across several real ales from independent local breweries which are located either within Exmoor itself or not far distant. Here is a potted guide to those breweries and their brews.

In the descriptions of the individual beers, OG stands for Original Gravity. That is a system of gauging the amount of fermentable sugars in the brew before the yeast is added and provides a rough indicator of strength. A more accurate guide to potency is provided by the ABV (Alcohol By Volume) figure. In both cases, the higher the figure, the stronger the beer.

Cotleigh Brewery, Ford Road, Wiveliscombe, Somerset TA4 2RE; Tel: (0984) 24086

Continued growth has taken this brewery a long way from its first home – a stable block at Cotleigh Farmhouse in 1979. Six years later, 1985 saw the completion of a purpose-built brewhouse and there was further expansion in 1991 with the purchase of adjoining premises and the doubling of brewing capacity. Most of the beers are seasonal or brewed for special occasions only. Serves 100 outlets, mostly in Devon and Somerset, although the beers are also available across the country. Owns one pub, the Prince of Wales in Holcombe Rogus, Devon, which was the East Devon CAMRA's Pub of the Year in 1992.

Harrier SPA	(OG 1036, ABV 3.6%) A straw-coloured beer with a very hoppy aroma and flavour, and a hoppy, bitter finish. Plenty of flavour for a light, low gravity beer.
Nutcracker Mild	(OG 1036, ABV 3.8%) A dark mild, an occasional brew.
Tawny Bitter	(OG 1040, ABV 3.8%) A mid brown-coloured, very consistent beer. A hoppy aroma, a hoppy but quite well-balanced flavour, and a hoppy, bitter finish.

Aldercote Ale

(OG 1042, ABV 4.2%) An occasional brew for East-West Ales wholesalers.

Barn Owl Bitter

(OG 1048, ABV 4.5%) Brewed only occasionally, in aid of the brewery's adopted charity, the Hawk and Owl Trust.

Old Buzzard

(OG 1048, ABV 4.8%) Dark ruby-red beer, tasting strongly of roast malt, balanced with hops. Roast malt again in the finish, with bitterness. Very drinkable once the taste is acquired.

Rebellion

(OG 1050, ABV 5%) An occasional brew.

Red Nose Reinbeer

(OG 1060, ABV 5.6%) A dark and warming Christmas brew.

Exmoor Ales Ltd, Golden Hill Brewery, Wiveliscombe, Somerset TA4 2NY; Tel: (0984) 23798

When it first started production in 1980, this brewery won immediate national acclaim, with its Exmoor Ale winning the Best Bitter award at CAMRA's Great British Beer Festival. Operating from the former Hancock's Brewery at Wiveliscombe (closed 1959), it now supplies real ale to some 150 pubs in the region and a wholesale network covering virtually the whole country. No houses of its own. A new addition to the range is Exmoor Beast, a winter ale.

Exmoor Ale

(OG 1039, ABV 3.8%) Pale brown beer with a malty aroma and a malty, dry taste. Bitter and malty finish. Very drinkable.

Exmoor Gold

(OG 1045, ABV 4.5%) Yellow/golden in colour, with a malty aroma and flavour, and a slight sweetness and hoppiness. Sweet, malty finish.

Exmoor Stag	(OG 1050, ABV 5.2%) Pale brown beer, with a malty taste and aroma, and a bitter finish. Slightly sweet. Very similar to Exmoor Ale and drinks as easily.
Exmoor Beast	(OG 1066, ABV 6.6%) A winter brew: October-March.

Ushers Brewery Ltd, Parade House, Trowbridge, Wilts, BA14 8JF; Tel: (0225) 763171

Along with Ruddles, another recent escapee from the Grand Metropolitan/Courage net. This West Country brewery was founded in 1824, but lost its identity after being swallowed up by Watney in 1960. A successful management buy-out in 1992 has given Ushers back its independence and the once-famous Founders Ale is now brewed again in Wiltshire. The old Pale Ale may also be re-introduced. Supplies real ale to virtually all its 437 tied houses and to Courage/Grand Met Inntrepreneur pubs.

Best Bitter	(OG 1037, ABV 3.8%) Cleaner-tasting than its lack-lustre Grand Met predecessor, with gentle malt and hops but a harsh bitter dryness. Drinks light for a best bitter but, at the time of sampling, the brewery were still working on the beer.
Founders Ale	(OG 1044, ABV 4.5%)

Wadworth & Co Ltd, Northgate Brewery, Devizes, Wilts, SN10 1JW; Tel: (0380) 723361

Delightful market town brewery set up in 1885 by Henry Wadworth. Solidly traditional, the brewery still runs horse-drawn drays. The brewery has recently undergone some expansion with the installation of new fermenting vessels to cope with increased demand from the free trade – some 500 outlets are now supplied directly by the brewery, and over 3,000 more via other brewers and wholesalers. Always keen to expand the tied estate (currently 182 houses, all of which offer real ale).

6X remains one of the South's most famous ales, whilst Henry Wadworth IPA is now called Henry's Original IPA.

Henry's Original IPA

(OG 1034, ABV 3.8%) A golden brown-coloured beer with a gentle, malty and slightly hoppy aroma, a good balance of flavours, with maltiness gradually dominating, and then a long-lasting aftertaste to match, eventually becoming biscuity. A good session beer, more pleasing than the popular 6X.

6X

(OG 1040, ABV 4.3%) Mid brown in colour, with a malty and fruity nose and some balancing hop character. The flavour is similar, with some bitterness and a lingering malty but bitter finish. Full-bodied and distinctive.

Farmer's Glory

(OG 1046, ABV 4.5%) Can be delightfully hoppy and fruity, but is variable in flavour and conditioning. The aroma is of malt and it should have a dryish, hoppy aftertaste.

Old Timer

(OG 1055, ABV 5.8%) Available in winter only. A rich, copper-brown beer with a strong fruity, malty aroma. The flavour is full-bodied and complete, with hints of butterscotch and peaches, beautifully balanced by a lasting, malty, dry finish. A classic beer.

(With acknowledgments and thanks to the Campaign for Real Ale, CAMRA, and their 'Good Beer Guide'.)

More Information

There is a chain of information centres spread across the Exmoor National Park although they tend to open only at peak times.

Dulverton (tel: 0398 23841/23665).
Dunster (tel: 0643 821835).
County Gate, Countisbury (tel: 05987 321).
Lynmouth (tel: 0598 52509).
Combe Martin (tel: 0271 883319).

Postal enquiries should be addressed to the Exmoor National Park Information Centre, Exmoor House, Dulverton, Somerset.

The Exmoor National Park Ranger Service are always ready and willing to give advice, guidance and practical assistance to walkers and other visitors. They can be contacted by telephoning any of the following numbers:

0643 706612; 0643 841512; 0643 862328; 0643 862788; 0769 572216

Further Reading

Exmoor National Park by Glyn Court, published by Michael Joseph

The Visitor's Guide to Somerset, Dorset & Wiltshire by Alan Proctor, published by Moorland

A Visitor's Guide to the National Parks of England & Wales by John Wyatt, published by Michael Joseph

Ordnance Survey Landranger Guidebook to North Devon, Exmoor & the Quantocks, compiled by Peter Titchmarsh, published by Jarrold

Ordnance Survey Leisure Guide to Devon & Exmoor, published by the OS and Automobile Association

Exmoor & The Quantocks by John Earle, published by Cicerone Press

WALKS 1 & 2: DUNSTER

Route 1: Dunster Castle, Carhampton Gate, Broadwood Farm, Towns Wood, Avill Farm, Hole's Corner, St Leonard's Well, Old Park

Route 2: Dunster Steep, The Yarn Market, The Nunnery, Spears Cross, Gallox Bridge, The Village Pound, The Dovecote, Exmoor Visitor Centre

Distance: route 1, 8 miles; route 2, 1.5 miles

Map: Ordnance Survey Pathfinder 1215 (SS 84/94)

Start: *Route 1:* Gallox Bridge. Pathfinder map reference 989432; *Route 2:* Steep car park. Pathfinder map reference 993439

How to get there: Dunster, on the north eastern edge of Exmoor and well signposted, is located on the A396 at its junction with the A39, 3 miles south east of Minehead.

The Pubs

This fascinating village offers a choice of four real ale watering holes which, together with the wealth of interest in the area, make it an appropriate location for, dare I say it, a pub crawl.

The Forester's Arms is a large drinking house on the southern edge of Dunster and, because of its location away from the centre, less frequented by tourists perhaps. The 15th century Stag's Head, closer to the castle, has a reputation for a friendly atmosphere. Both have their own individual appeal.

I recommend the **Dunster Castle Hotel** (tel: 0643 821445) for sound practical reasons: it's the only one open all day. Which counts for a lot at the end of a long (or even a short) thirst-making walk which finishes in the middle of the afternoon, as mine did. The modern lounge and cellar bars may lack atmosphere – this is definitely not a rural retreat. But you are spared the hunt mementoes – pictures, paintings and paraphernalia –

which are a common feature of the vast majority of Exmoor pubs. There is a no smoking area too, no bad thing. You can get something to eat all day long, including vegetarian dishes. Children are welcome, although there is no family room.

Most important of all, what about the beer? This free house had Flowers Original and Boddingtons Bitter handpumped by beer engine when I went quaffing. Other facilities include accommodation, a garden bar well away from the busy high street, entertainment comprising pool, darts and music; plus plenty of car parking round the back. And it's all almost literally in the shadow of the castle itself.

The Dunster Castle Hotel, with the castle itself beyond.

My other choice was the **Luttrell Arms** (tel: 0643 821555), another free house only this time part of the THF Trusthouse Forte hotels group. The ivy clad building, right opposite Dunster's historic Yarn Market, is itself steeped in history. Dating back to the 15th century, it started life as a guest house for the monks of nearby Cleeve Abbey, becoming an inn called The Ship in the mid 1600s. The current name was adopted in 1779, doubtless to curry favour with the next door neighbour, the Lord of the Manor in Dunster castle. (In fact the Luttrell family were resident in the castle for exactly 600 years, 1376 – 1976, when the National Trust took over.)

The Luttrell Arms back bar boasts what has been described as a 'pubby atmosphere'. It certainly has character. The bar, with its old settles, high beams and ancient black timber, 12-light window frame, looks out on a small, enclosed, galleried courtyard through wavy, hand-floated glass, itself an object of considerable interest.

If you have an historical bent, you will doubtless appreciate the 17th century plasterwork of Dutch origin, the loopholed porch tower and the medieval hall with hammer beam roof. If not, just sit back and enjoy the draught Bass, Whitbread or Flowers IPA on handpump. Or sample the steak & kidney & claret pie. Snacks and full meals are served both at lunchtime and in the evening. The 5.30pm opening time (at least in the summer) compensates to an extent at least for the afternoon's closed doors.

The Walks

Route 1 starts at the pay-&-display car park next to Gallox Bridge. As you walk towards this medieval packhorse bridge you pass what will be many people's idea of the ideal place of retirement, the aptly named Rose Cottage. Just beyond the bridge is a less appetising site, a crossroads where once stood the gallows from which it gained its name.

At the crossroads take the track to the left, heading south east, signposted Withycombe and Carhampton. It sports a red waymark.

Almost immediately you cross a stile complete with dog gate and come to another signpost where you head straight on towards Carhampton. A swarm of shimmering dragonflies provided an escort when I passed this way, which offers one of the best views possible of the castle.

The track is wide and clearly defined, the soil underfoot that rich red colour so typical of the West Country. Listen out for the whistle of a steam train. It will come from the West Somerset Light Railway which runs into Minehead from near Taunton, about 16 miles away.

Pass through one gateway and continue in the same direction until you reach Carhampton Gate, where you turn right, south westwards, onto a wide, stony bridlepath heading gently uphill. This is like a sunken road, lined on one side by a dry stone wall-based hedgerow and on the other by a parade of tall trees, probably planted by the Knight family who did so much in the 19th century to open up Exmoor.

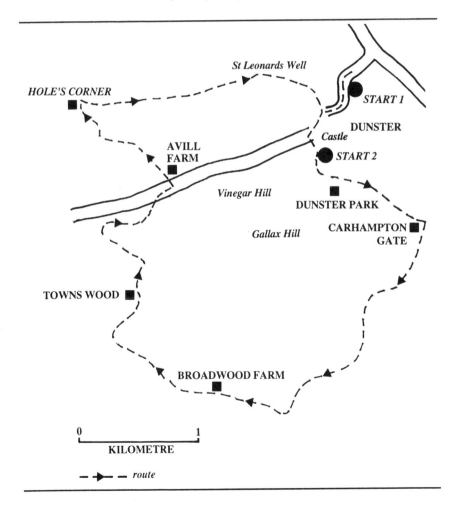

St Leonards Well

HOLE'S CORNER

START 1

DUNSTER

AVILL FARM

Castle

START 2

Vinegar Hill

DUNSTER PARK

Gallax Hill

CARHAMPTON GATE

TOWNS WOOD

BROADWOOD FARM

0   1
KILOMETRE

route

Ignore forks to left and right, the waymarks at Withycombe Hill Gate too, and stick with the wall-cum-hedgerow. As the track, having reached its high point among the trees, begins to descend, you will see ahead the crest of Croydon Hill, at 365m one of the local high spots. Over to the left (south-southeast), the roofs of Gupworthy Farm can be seen peeping out among the trees.

After passing the right fork leading to Kings Hedge Coppice, turn left down a narrower, overgrown track, heading south west. That links up with another sunken lane which can be muddy in wet weather. At the hairpin, ignore the waymarks and the temptation to stick to the beaten track. Turn sharp right across the stream and head west north west. Be prepared for it to be boggy here and don't be put off by the undergrowth and overgrowth.

Beyond the gate, head westwards; follow the hedgerow as the path is barely visible on the ground. You are now out in the open on a hillside but with solid banks of trees on the skyline all the way round the compass. Continuing on in the same direction through another gateway brings you to a third where you join a lane by a footpath sign. That leads you through Broadwood Farm, after which a left fork where the lane hairpins right puts you back among the trees.

Continuing on, climbing gently, eventually brings you to the lane at Nutcombe Bottom, thence, beyond the lane, Towns Wood and Whits Wood. A diversion was in force here. Don't bother climbing up through the trees to the crest of Whits Wood hill but swing left or right around the base, going either clockwise or anti-clockwise so as to emerge from the trees on the hillside above Avill Farm, where you cross the A396.

Heading north-north west, follow the unsignposted farm track past some cottages. A footbridge alongside a ford takes you across the Avill to a narrow lane which you also cross. Then start climbing. This is Avill Ball and only one word springs to mind as an accurate description of the path: steep.

You get your reward at the top. After that ascent through the trees, Hole's Corner (odd name), is like an eagle's eyrie. What a view. The Welsh coastline is clearly visible across the Bristol Channel.

Having regained your breath and drunk your fill of the view, head eastwards along the top of the ridge so that you can drink your fill in a more literal way in Dunster, which lies ahead. It's all downhill from here on in. Just bear left at the forks and keep heading eastwards. That will bring you to the outskirts of the village and Conduit Lane. Now, with four pubs to choose from at which to slake your thirst, you can't go wrong.

Route 2 also involves lots of climbing – but only of the pavement along the High Street and, if you so wish, the steps up into the four real ale hostelries already mentioned.

Start at the public car park in Dunster Steep, which is not at all intimidating, despite its name. It is possible to leave your car without charge in the Old Park. That is National Trust property with access via a rather imposing archway and drive reached via Loxhole Bridge on the A39. A public footpath links the park, which is ideal for a family picnic, with the village centre. Better still, join the National Trust and pay your way: there are plenty of benefits, including free admission to the castle grounds and gardens.

As you head up the Steep, make a detour into the Exmoor National Park Visitor Centre. It's well worth a visit.

The Luttrell Arms guards the entrance to the High Street. The ivy is so thick on the walls you get the impression that it wasn't built of bricks at all. In fact part was originally constructed from stone salvaged from the battlements of Dunster castle after a particularly fierce medieval battle. Avoid the temptation to wet your whistle (all right, wet it, wet it). Either way, take a look at the quaint old Yarn Market opposite, one of the most distinctive features in a village full of the distinctive.

This eight-sided, open walled building dates back to the 17th century. Here it was that local people gathered to sell woollen goods in general and Dunsters, a local, soft kersey cloth, in particular. Spot the hole in one of the rafters made by a cannon ball fired during the siege of the castle in the Civil War.

At the other end of the High Street, which was originally known rather more colourfully as the Shambles, is our second watering hole, the

Dunster Castle Hotel. Bear in mind that this walk has only just started and that there are still two real ale pubs to go. . .

Before turning the corner below the castle into Church Street, glance back up the Shambles. The main street is unusually wide and dominated at the northern end by what look like the battlements of another castle. The structure peeping out of the hilltop trees is in fact a folly, Conygar Tower, built in 1776. (There must be something significant locally about dates ending in 76. . .) Appropriately enough so far as we are concerned, the expense of building it included £54, an enormous sum then, for the workmen's cider.

The road narrows markedly to squeeze past the old Nunnery which, despite its name, was never used as such. Dating back to the 15th century, jettied and tile hung, it gives all the appearance now of being three separate cottages but was originally one house.

Heading westwards, down West Street (where else), you pass on your left the Spears Cross Hotel (whose round is it this time?). A document dating back to 1486 refers to a 'dwelling house of William Sper standing opposite the cross'. The pub itself dates from the same period.

Cross the road and you come to the Stag's Head mentioned earlier. Now could be the time to check out that friendly atmosphere I referred to. Or perhaps not.

Back on the southern side of West Street is a turning leading to the river and Gallox Bridge. On a warm day it's refreshing to dangle your hands and feet in the fast-flowing water in the raised leat which feeds the mill at the lower end of the lane.

West Street offers more refreshment in the form of the Forester's Arms, another of our chosen quorum of quaffing places. Further on, you can view a 17th century longhouse-style thatched cottage with circular chimney, one of the oldest in the area. Further on still, and the furthest point of our Dunster stroll, are the remains of the 17th century village pound.

Retrace your steps, this time taking to the backstreets via 'Rattle Row Ancient road', now renamed St Thomas Street. En route, pause to admire the superb wagon roof on the 15th century priory church of St George.

And listen out for the tuneful bells, a peal of eight and a carillon which plays a different tune each day. The nearby Norman dovecote used to be home to 500 birds, would you believe. When times were hard, the revolving wooden ladder inside enabled the locals to stock up on the ingredients for pigeon pie.

Follow the road and you will find yourself back at the Luttrell Arms. Where, if you are so inclined, you can start all over again. . .

Dunster Castle peeps throught the trees – this is route one.

WALK 3: WITHYPOOL

Route: Tarr Steps, Parsonage Down, Worth Lane, Withypool, Uppington
Plantation, Oakbeer Wood, Lea Wood, Knaplock Wood, Tarr Farm

Distance: about 8 miles (detour reduces to about 4 miles)

Map: Ordnance Survey Pathfinder 1235 (SS 83/93)

Start: Tarr Steps car park, Pathfinder map reference 872323

How to get there: Tarr Steps is located in the southern half of Exmoor
midway between Dulverton and Exford. From the B3223, which links up
with the A396 in the east and the A39 well over to the west, follow signs
westwards to the Steps.

The Pub

The Royal Oak (a familiar name on Exmoor) is a real huntin', shootin',
fishin' pub and popular with the walkin' fraternity too. Witness the
number of pairs of boots lined up by the door of the Rod Room Bar. I
saw more ramblers here than at any other watering hole in this national
park. That's doubtless because they recognise a real rural retreat when
they see one.

This inn (tel: 064 383 506) is a favourite with the eatin' set as well.
Escargots were just one of the specialities on the restaurant menu. Those
snails plus a wine list more than 70 labels long give a flavour of what
you can expect, but, so far as the restaurant is concerned, only in the
evening. Lunchtime, suppertime too, bar meals are the order of the day.
Try the Danish open shrimp sandwich with six giant prawns, the
Somerset pasties or the home cured ham.

The atmosphere in the two bars, with their oak beams, memorabilia and
inevitable hunt trophies as well as tally ho hunting scenes galore, is cosy.
The log fires in stone fireplaces help. So too do the real ales available on
draught: Exmoor Ale and Ushers Best Bitter pulled by hand pump.
Vintage brandies and malt whiskies are a speciality too. But don't expect

any special facilities for the family. In fact, youngsters under ten are not allowed in the accommodation which this inn offers although, strangely, dogs are. On warm, sunny days, walkers with children could use the wooden benches and tables with parasols on the terrace while quenching their thirst.

The author of 'Lorna Doone', R. D. Blackmore, stayed at the Royal Oak in 1866 while writing his famous novel. In fact the inn dates back further than that: approximately three centuries. A safari-full of huntin', shootin' etc can be arranged here, including horse riding. But don't be tempted. By the time you reach the Royal Oak, you will be half way round the walk which follows and it would be a shame to miss the riverside route back to your starting point.

The Walk

The lane leading down to Tarr Steps can get congested at touristy times so don't be tempted to drive all the way down to the river. Pull into the car park and start strolling. A waymarked route through the fields alongside the lane avoids the need to tramp the tarmac.

Tarr Steps: 17 spans, 10 stone slabs – a clapper bridge par excellence.

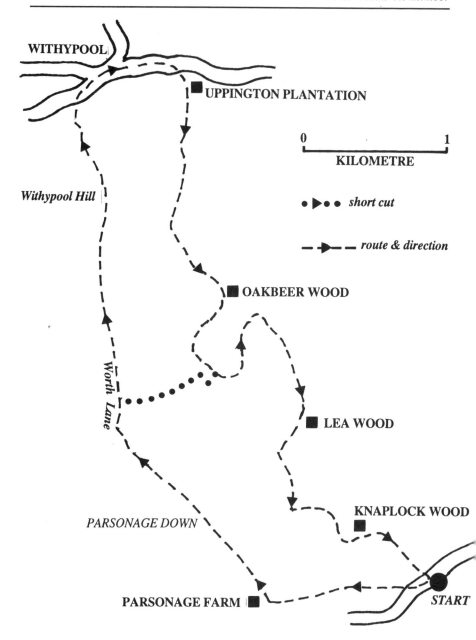

The 17 spans of the 165ft-long Tarr Steps are a striking sight. The stones which make up this, the longest and, arguably, finest clapper bridge in England, each weighs up to ten tons. Nonetheless, more than once the structure has been damaged and even swept away by the Barle flooding its banks. The current bridge, of unknown age but believed to date back to medieval times, was rebuilt by the Royal Engineers in 1961.

On the far side of the river, the route is signposted Withypool Hill 2.5 miles and sports a yellow waymark. The tarmac soon gives way to a stony sunken lane which winds its way uphill before changing into grass and crossing three fields, rising virtually all the way. You swing right (north west) just before a farm gate, signposted Withypool Hill. This is part of the Two Moors Way. Having crossed three more fields, you begin to descend, with Westwater Farm clearly visible ahead and below. There are yellow waymarks all the way. Many of the trees on this leg of the walk were a mass of red berries when I passed by. (Indicating a cold winter?) A metal gate gives access to Worth Lane alongside a quaint little roadbridge, all moss, ivy and time-weathered stone.

Follow the lane, part of the Two Moors Way, into Withypool. It rises quite steeply at first. On this hilly section, according to the OS map, there is a public right of way running due east at Worth which links up with the riverside route below. Although it is not signposted nor waymarked, I made my way across the fields down to the riverbank. You can turn the walk into a figure of eight or cut it in half by using this link. But be prepared to paddle across the river because there are no stepping stones nor footbridge.

Back on Worth Lane, following a cattle grid you come out onto the open moorland of Withypool Hill. To your left, the bleak, brown moor above; to your right, the green and wooded river valley below. Quite a contrast.

And so to Withypool itself and the Royal Oak Inn. . .

Afterwards, follow (stagger?) the road eastwards uphill out of the village until you can cut through the hedgerow on your right at a stile signposted 'riverside walk' and featuring more of those yellow waymarks. Superb views down the river valley it provides too.

A steep downhill section brings you to said riverside walk. Twisting and turning, rising and falling, it meanders its way back, faithfully following the Barle, to your starting point. And throughout, yellow waymarks to keep you on course. En route there are fords and footbridges large and small, stepping stones, detours if you wish to make them and diversions.

To avoid the need for a river crossing near Great Bradley, a permissive path has been established with the cooperation of the local landowner. So although the public right of way runs on the western bank, you stay on the eastern side. The diversion makes life simpler.

Watery Lane provides a detour to Knaplock if you feel the need. Otherwise the walk continues, mainly through broadleaf woodland, light, airy and sunny, along the riverside back to Tarr Steps. But not before passing what looks at first glance like a rope-walk across the Barle. No, this is not part of a commando assault course. It is in fact a cable debris-arrester, sited upstream of the old clapper bridge so as to intercept floating logs and prevent them damaging the structure as has happened in the past.

No, not part of an assault course, but a river debris-arrester

WALK 4: PORLOCK

Route: Porlock, West Luccombe, Buddle Hill, Selworthy, Selworthy Beacon, Bossington Hill, Lynch Combe, Bossington, Sparkhayes

Distance: about 9 miles

Map: Ordnance Survey Pathfinder 1215 (SS 84/94)

Start: Doverhay car park, Pathfinder map reference 882467

How to get there: Porlock is top dead centre, towards the northern edge of Exmoor and only a mile or so from the coast. The A39, linking Lynton and Minehead, goes slap bang through the centre of the village.

The Pubs

Two from which to choose, both in the main street, both real ale watering holes, both offering family rooms. But there the significant similarities end and the differences begin to make themselves evident.

The Castle (tel: 0643 862504) is a large, renovated hotel. The large single bar in this free house has the atmosphere of a drinking man's (and woman's) pub, busy and bustling. On draught when I visited were a choice of Tetley Bitter, Bass and Courage Best with cider an option at peak periods. As well as the pool tables, darts and, at certain times only, skittles – they have their own indoor skittle alley – you will also find, dare I say it, fruit machines and a juke box. An open fire, assorted games trophies, an interesting collection of mounted fag-cards, sorry, cigarette cards, and horse brasses provide decoration. You can get bar snacks as well as full meals – a room is set aside. The hot potato snackettes available free over the bar are tasty. But be warned that parking at holiday times can be difficult.

The same comment applies, only more so, to the **Royal Oak** (tel: 0643 862798), which dates back to 1704. Apparently smaller from the outside, it is deceptively roomy inside with one bar only but several semi-separate sections.

Regarded by people who live in the area as a 'lively village local', it's more of a family pub, perhaps, than its neighbour – certainly there were far more families with children when I visited than in the Castle. The choice of draught beer is wider too: Ruddles Best Bitter, Courage Directors and Best, Websters Yorkshire Bitter and Ushers Best Bitter, all on hand pump. Again, cider on draught is an option at touristy times. Likewise you will find a juke box, fruit machine and pool table. The landlord here is keen on his trophies too.

The usual snacks and meals are served but the menu does at least include some vegetarian as well as children's dishes.

The Walk

Be prepared to pay when parking in Porlock in the summer. Its narrow winding streets were not designed with late-20th century motoring in mind. Car space is at a premium, with too many of the former and too little of the latter. Which makes it all the pleasanter to get out of the village, interesting as it is, away from the hustle and bustle.

Doverhay provides a good start for a walk too, with its 15th century museum and information centre, cluster of pretty thatched cottages and little lanes with quaint names such as The Drang (whatever one of those is. . .) and Bond's Row. As you climb steadily, notice the hedgerow on your left and the carefully and intricately built drystone wall which forms its foundation. Following a cattle grid, the lane, still climbing, passes the Porlock water treatment works on your right and presents clear views across the water of Porlock Bay on your left.

Descending now and after crossing a second cattle grid, you pass another cluster of cream-washed, thatched cottages before arriving at West Luccombe and the ancient, cobbled packhorse bridge over Horner Water – a slightly more modern version carries cars across the stream.

Our route up and over the fields is signposted Holnicote. A series of such signposts guides you across six fields, several stiles, a gaggle of gates plus a lane and a footbridge to Holnicote House. Part way, you will notice on the hillside straight ahead a large, white building. This useful navigation aid is in fact Selworthy church, which we come to later.

Skirt Holnicote House eastwards until you reach a signposted gate leading through the grounds, which boast some luxuriant shrubs and plants, not to mention a magnificent cedar of Lebanon tree. The house used to be a holiday home for the Acland family. It has burnt down three times since the end of the 18th century – strange. . . Leaving the grounds and colourful flower displays behind, cross Buddle Hill (careful, this is the A39) and follow the lane leading up to Selworthy.

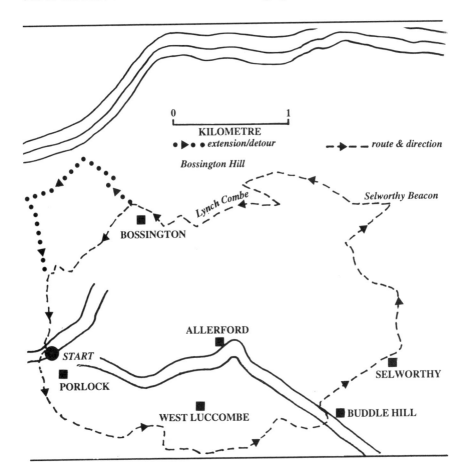

This picture book village is the natural haunt of the species 'touristus visitorum' and you can expect to find large numbers, gabbling noisily, during the summer months. They are relatively harmless but don't disturb them.

The cream-washed, thatched cottages date back to 1810 and were built by local baronet Sir Thomas Acland as retirement homes for some of his workforce. They are grouped around a communal green, all honeysuckle and roses, with names like Greenacres and Glebe Cottage. They sport a nice line in apple trees too. That's not to mention the blocks of trees on the hillside beyond, each planted by Sir Thomas to celebrate the birth of one of his nine children.

Also in Selworthy is a plaque commemorating the 'first wanderings of Walter Wilkinson 1888 – 1970, Puppeteer and Author of the Peep Show'. And so to that church, All Saints, an example of Exmoor ecclesiastical building at its richest. Variously said to date back to the 15th or 17th century, it is crowned with a square embattled tower, possesses one of the finest wagon roofs in the West Country and has been blessed with what must be among the best views of any church in Christendom.

Follow the signposts towards Selworthy Beacon, up, up through Sir Thomas's woodland. Roe deer have been seen here. You are now into National Trust property, the path through the trees wide, sun dappled and clearly defined. It climbs steadily. Pause for a while and for breath in the memorial hut at the edge of the plantation and consider the words that have been inscribed on its walls. There is a lesson here for every walker. . .

Now the face of the landscape changes dramatically. You leave behind the fields and wooded combes and enter an area of open moorland, all heather, gorse, bracken and wide open skies. From Selworthy Beacon itself, 308m, the view is panoramic, the land dropping away steeply down to the sea to the north and equally steeply down to the valley bottom to the south. It's a real eagle's eyrie of a viewpoint.

You stay up high for a mile westwards before zigzagging downhill into Lynch Combe, the path clearly visible on the ground and signposted at regular intervals. Now Porlock, the mile-deep plain known as the Marsh separating it from the sea to which it was once attached and its grey shingle beach loom large ahead. So too does the coastline westward ho! It's steep, thickly wooded and devoid of sand. Not the place for a sun-sea-and-sand summer holiday but ideal walking country at any time of year.

At first skirting, then entering, the Allerford Plantation brings you via signposted paths and a charming little footbridge, across Horner Water once more, to Bossington, a pretty village nestling under the hill of the same name. A track leads down to the stony beach here. Normally the stream runs underneath the pebbles into the sea but in times of flood it bursts up through the stones with a mighty roar. Be warned.

You have a choice of routes for this final leg back to Porlock; via the beach or, the shorter route, direct, across the Marsh, which is in reality a network of fields. Either way, you end up at Sparkhayes. Skirting the housing estate brings you back to the centre of Porlock. If you didn't delve before you started the walk, don't miss a look at the 13th century St Dubricius' church, one of only four in the country dedicated to the Welsh saint. Its truncated spire and richly canopied tomb to Sir Simon FitzRoger, complete with full suit of armour, make it well worth the (small) detour. It is reached from Doverhay direct via The Drang.

WALK 5: DUNKERY BEACON

Route: Wootton Courtney, Dunkery Hill, Dunkery Beacon, Dunkery Gate, Spangate Land, Hole Cross, Ford, Wootton Courtney, Brockwell

Distance: 9 miles

Map: Ordnance Survey Pathfinder 1215 (SS 84/94)

Start: Brockwell, Pathfinder map reference 928432

How to get there: Wootton Courtney lies in the north eastern part of Exmoor, away from the main through roads. Coming from the north, turn southwards off the A39 midway between Minehead and Porlock. Approaching from the south, take one of the lanes heading northwards off the A396 near Timberscombe. In all cases, follow signs for Wootton.

The Pub

Not surprisingly you get the requisite views from the **Dunkery Beacon Hotel** in Wootton Courtney (tel: 064 384 241). And it isn't only Exmoor's highest point which is visible from this hillside watering hole. You may quaff your ale from the terrace with large parts of the moor spread out before you, the Brendon Hills too.

Proprietors Kenneth and Daphne Midwood can rightly lay claim to a genuine garden bar at this free house: the lawns are quite extensive. Just like the pink-washed building itself. Large and largely unmodernised, it rambles rather than stands, with chimneys seemingly all over the place and no shortage of space for parking or spreading yourself.

Inside, you can choose from between two bars and very different in character they are too. The public bar is all workmanlike, handmade, copper-topped tables, bar billiards and quarried floor tiles. Just right for walkers with muddy boots. The bar itself gives the impression of having travelled through time from an earlier age. And there's a large wood-burning stove, complete with inglenook type corner seats, to keep things cosy in the winter too.

Step next door into the lounge (no muddy boots please) and the atmosphere is much more genteel: polished wooden tables and tapestry covered settles. Either way you can avail yourself of a tankard or three of real ale. This watering hole was one of only two I came across on Exmoor at which it was served straight from a barrel behind the bar. Exmoor Ale from the local Golden Hill Brewery at nearby Wiveliscombe was the only brew on draught when I visited. But others may be on tap when you visit: Flowers IPA has been a favourite in the past.

Meals and snacks are available at lunchtimes and in the evenings. Children are catered for on the menu, which included such local delicacies as Dunkery Munchers and Dunkery Platters. (You can't really blame the landlord for cashing in on his local tourist attraction, can you.)

Needless to say, there is accommodation here if you require it. Theme weekends and activity holidays are a speciality, with topics on offer as

Archetypal country cottage at Ford, near Dunkery Beacon – beware of the dog!

diverse as shooting and painting. Depending upon your tastes, there is no shortage of suitable material for either, as the walk which follows demonstrates.

The Walk

No walking tour of Exmoor is complete without a visit to its highest point and Wootton Courtney supplies an ideal entree, one which emphasises Dunkery Beacon's high flying, wide open spaces. It does so by providing a starting point at Brockwell which initially hides all of that from you, springing its surprise and making the effect all the more dramatic.

This is National Trust territory and in typical NT style the route is nothing if not visible: signposted, waymarked and clearly defined. You start as you do not mean to go on – by plunging into a wood. But after several hundred yards that gives way to the open hillside, all heather and bracken, the sky above and the views all around. And the higher you go, the wider the panorama becomes, the track winding its way ahead like a ribbon.

It's a long, straight, steady though gentle climb up to the Beacon, two miles as both the crow flies and you will walk, due south west, 380 metres' rise in altitude. Underfoot, and unlikely to worry the crow although it could you, a stony track on which it would not be difficult to twist an ankle. Best save the Exmoor Ale till afterwards so that you are steady on your feet.

As I walked I suddenly noticed a lone horseman on the skyline. Shortly he disappeared. After a while a second materialised further along the ridge only to follow the first over the skyline. Minutes later came the sound of hooves behind me and a red-jacketed figure galloped by heading in the same direction. The next minute, over the crest of the hill came a line of red and black jacketed horsemen escorting a pack of dogs. Yes, you've guessed it: the hunt.

Dunkery is one of the haunts of Exmoor's native wild red deer. And therefore an area favoured by the Devon & Somerset Staghounds. I saw no sign of their quarry but there was no shortage of hunt followers. The closer I came to the road which skirts the Beacon, the more became

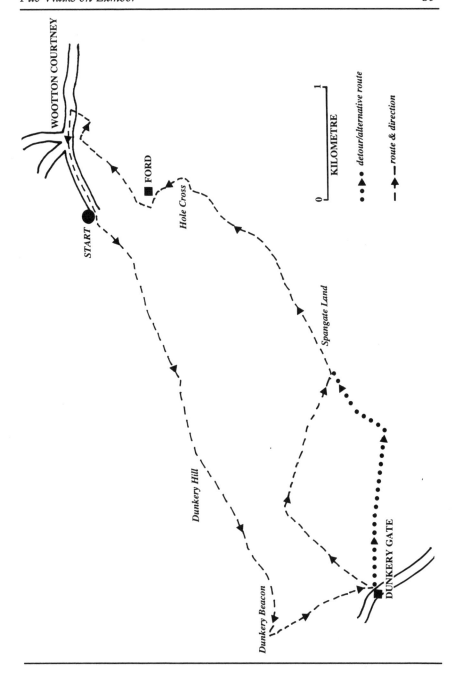

KILOMETRE

0   1

● ● ● ▲ ●   *detour/alternative route*

●   ▲   *route & direction*

WOOTTON COURTNEY

START

FORD

Hole Cross

Spangate Land

Dunkery Hill

Dunkery Beacon

DUNKERY GATE

visible. There must have been dozens of Land Rovers, Range Rovers and other, mainly four-wheel-drive, vehicles up there following the course of events. Fortunately only on the road I hasten to add.

A wide, even more clearly defined track leads the way from the road up to the Beacon itself. Footpath erosion here is only too evident so keep to the track and avoid making it any worse.

Two cairns and a threatened Ordnance Survey trig point mark Exmoor's highest point. At 519m above sea level and 100m higher than most of the rest of the moor, Dunkery acts as a magnet for walkers and other visitors. And there are no prizes for guessing why. On an outstandingly clear day you can see the Pembrokeshire Coast National Park; the Gower Peninsula with the Cambrian Mountains, Brecon Beacons and Black Mountains beyond; the Forest of Dean, the Malvern Hills, the Cotswolds; the Blackdown Hills on the Devon border; Dartmoor; Brown Willy and Rough Tor on Bodmin Moor in Cornwall; perhaps even, dimly to the south, the English Channel.

The author on a high: Dunkery Beacon, complete with cairn.

No wonder it was chosen as a signal station. Beacon fires used to be lit here at times of national importance or danger. Nowadays they are used to celebrate special events, such as royal weddings, jubilees and, as in 1969, the centenary of Blackmore's 'Lorna Doone'.

Drink your fill of the view. Add a stone maybe to the impromptu cairn. Swap experiences with the other walkers. Then take the south eastern track, one of several which radiate from the Beacon like the spokes of a wheel, down to Dunkery Gate and Dunkery Bridge.

Here, you could, if you wished, take the bridle path running more or less parallel to the River Avill through Bincombe Wood and Dunkery Errish. An easier to follow route is north eastwards along the road for a few hundred yards to a signpost for Wheddon Cross where you head downhill on a broad track across the heather heading south east. Either way, you pass through a gateway near a signpost ('Wootton Courtney 2.5 miles) at the foot of the open moorland to enter a field which is known as Spangate Land. There is no footpath evident on the ground so head north east, maintaining your height, until you find yourself alongside a hedgerow beyond another gate. Follow that, keeping it on your left, and you come to a sunken lane. But not before the church and the white and pink washed buildings of Wootton Courtney come into clear view ahead.

It's all downhill from here to Hole Cross, with the sunken lane becoming almost a sunken tunnel at the end, so overgrown are the trees and hedgerows. A signpost confirms the route, a hairpin left turn by a lane at Hole Cross. Be prepared for a deeply rutted, muddy track here. At Ford where, perhaps needless to say, there is a ford, complete with pretty little flagstone footbridge, this latest sunken lane becomes a proper tarmac lane. It passes a pretty thatched cottage guarded by several very noisy dogs before climbing through a hairpin bend into woodland. These are the same woods we passed through at the start of the walk.

Continuing along this lane would bring you back to Brockwell. But Wootton Courtney and the Dunkery Beacon Hotel lie just half a mile over to the east. . . A signposted stile points the way across the fields via Brookside Farm. It brings you to a village of sandstone buildings, population 238, which straggles more than a mile along the lower slopes of Wootton Common. The 13th century church is worth a visit, before or after the Beacon Hotel.

WALKS 6 & 7: EXFORD

Route 1: Exford, River Exe, Stone Cross, Stone Down, Sharcott, Coombe Farm, Exford

Route 2: Exford, River Exe, North Higher Combe, Staddon Farm, East & West Nethercote, Lyncombe, Monk Cross, Exford

Distance: *route 1*, 3.5 miles; *route 2*, 7 miles

Map: Ordnance Survey Pathfinder 1235 (SS 83/93)

Start: *Routes 1 & 2:* Exford car park, Pathfinder map reference 854383

How to get there: Exford is almost at the centre of Exmoor, on the B3224, just to the east of its junction with the B3223. Together, these two roads bisect Exmoor, linking up the A396 with the A39. Heading east or west, you can't miss it.

The Pubs

Two walks and two pubs to go with them. Both are in the centre of the village of Exford, both are large, long established inns as well as watering holes, both are under the same ownership. But in atmosphere and character they differ surprisingly markedly.

The Crown (tel: 064 383 554) is the quieter of the two. Overlooking the village green, it gives the impression of being more hotel than pub, with a simpler bar which had draught Ruddles Best Bitter on hand pump when I called. Ushers Best Bitter has been a favourite too. A feature log fireplace divides the bar into two and there are mementoes on the wall, including a few of the inevitable hunt trophies.

The building itself dates back to the 17th century, apparently, when it was a coaching inn. There is extensive stabling for guests' horses. At Christmas the traditional Boxing Day meet of the Devon & Somerset

Staghounds is held here. Obviously a popular haunt of the hunting fraternity.

A fairly simple menu of bar meals and snacks is always on offer although you could always go the whole hog and take a table in the restaurant for something more elaborate in the evening. With a cellar of 60 wines from which to choose, that is doubtless the best time – after your walk. Morning coffee and cream teas are available if you arrive too early in the morning or after lunchtime when the bar is closed. The attractive streamside garden, set in three acres of land, is a popular feature on warm, sunny days. Parking is no problem at all.

The White Horse, two minutes' walk away and fronting the River Exe, had an altogether busier and more bustling atmosphere when I supped here. But be warned that they cater for coach parties, when it can get very busy.

This even larger hostelry dates back even further, to the 16th century, although the main enlargement didn't take place until the 1800s. There are two bars, lengthy affairs, all local stone and beer barrels. Walls are covered with mementoes and memorabilia, pictures and prints, trophies of the hunt, all sorts. There's no doubt about the popularity of the Staghounds here.

Choice was the name of the game in the real ale stakes when I called: Flowers Original, Boddington Bitter, Cotleigh Tawny and Exmoor Gold were all on hand pump plus, a special offer, Royal Wessex. Take your pick. As with the Crown, morning coffee and cream teas are served. The snacks and meals menu is extensive: you can spend a good while just savouring the dishes chalked up on the large blackboard over the food bar. Shellfish is a speciality here. Children are catered for too.

All in all, there's a warm atmosphere at the White Horse (tel: 064 383 229) and one which doesn't come just from the log fire.

The Walks

To go with the brace of good pubs in this, the widely accepted capital of Exmoor, a brace of good walks. One ambles twice as far as the other. But you can if you wish combine the two to form a 10-mile figure-of-eight

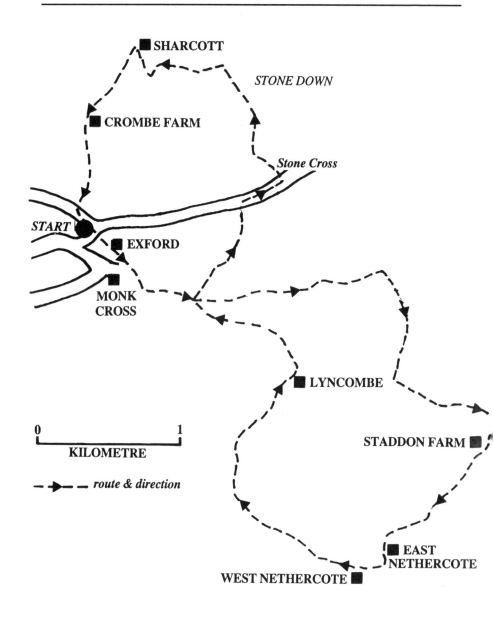

route or cut even shorter the shorter walk if the fancy takes you. No shortage of permutations here.

The shared starting point is a free car park in the centre of the village, right alongside the Exe. Both follow the riverbank and red waymarks through two kissing gates, followed by a gentle climb, signposted Winsford, to another gate, which you ignore, and a stile, which you climb. This is the parting of the ways.

Route 1:

Now the waymarks are yellow.

As you climb the fields, notice how the countryside contrasts with the bleak moorland higher up and through which you had to drive in order to reach Exford. Here, it's much gentler, softer, cultivated farmland. Compare it with the brown topped moors on the skyline above and behind.

Just before a gate which gives access to a sunken lane, pause once more to admire the view across the valley of the Exe, the longest river on Exmoor. Over to the east is the oddly named Broom Ball at just about the same height as you are now: 325m. Descending the lane (it can be very muddy here), you join the B3224 for a short stretch before turning up into Stone Lane via a rather imposing gateway – don't be put off. You soon discover where this track obtained its name: it is as if a giant had laid down a natural stone pavement or cobbled track.

Beyond the metal gate giving access to Stone and Prescott Downs, turn westwards and head downhill for a short distance, regaining height to reach Sharcott farm. Here, after passing through the midst of the farm buildings, you effectively make a hairpin turn. You will know you are on the right track if you leave the pond to your right and head downhill. A stile followed by a footbridge take you across a stream which you then follow to Coombe Farm.

The right of way passes through the centre of the farmyard (don't worry: the dogs are friendly) to link up with a wide, firm track which in fact is the driveway into the farm. At the far end, a short cut takes you across the fields. Not for the first time, the distinctive tower of St Mary Magdalene's church on the outskirts of the village will serve as a navigation beacon leading you down into Exford near the Police House. On the way back to the car park, you pass the village green, formerly used for sheep auctioning and known as The Fair Meadow. Then you will find yourself right by the front door of the Crown. . .

Route 2:

Follow the route as before, but at the gate and stile junction take the former rather than the latter this time. Red waymarks rule the route again as you make your way across first one field, then a second and a third to reach and cross a miniature combe complete with plank footbridge. Beyond the next field, now rising ground, the track you join is wide and firm enough for vehicles serving the farms here and at Lyncombe: follow the sign for Winsford via Staddon Hill.

You now climb steadily for the next mile or so as you follow Staddonhill Road which, I hasten to add, although metalled, is not subject to motorised traffic in any quantity. Just 20m short of the crest, which is 386m high, you swing sharply south eastwards. Which is as good an opportunity as any for pausing a while to soak up the 180-degree view. It's well worth absorbing. Notice in particular the patchwork quilt of fields and the way that it abruptly gives way to open, unfenced, solid brown moorland once it reaches a certain height.

Continuing on, you pass through Staddon Farm. The farm track, just before a metal gate, is not waymarked, nor signposted and looks private but a right of way runs through here nonetheless. Don't be put off.

Now begins your descent to the banks of the Exe, through several fields and gates, a sunken lane or two, muddy in places. The first you know of the river is the tinkling of a feeder stream just above the Nethercotes. Here, beyond a cluster of buildings and after crossing a stream, you enter some woodland running alongside and above the river.

Ignore the red arrows pointing off towards a footbridge over the Exe. We stick to the north bank of the river as it flows through steep, bracken covered Curr Cleeve.

After the open hilltops earlier, this is a real contrast, the pleasantest of woodland and riverside walks, with sunlight filtering through the broadleaf trees, the sound of the river just below. Red waymarks accompany you on your way as the route follows the meandering course of the river around the base of Lyncombe Hill heading back towards Exford.

Over on the opposite bank, on top of another hill, are some earthworks, the site of the Iron Age Road Castle. You can see why its builders chose this as its location; the site stands sentinel over the surrounding countryside and oversees a long stretch of the river.

The route here is wide, clearly defined and marked at regular intervals by gates. So you come to Lyncombe and another farmyard after which you change colours, go for yellow and fork left (north west). Shadow the course of the river until, shortly, you find yourself back at your starting point, the junction with the stile and gate. From there, it is a short distance back around the hill to the bridge over the Exe leading to Court Farm, which you bypass, and Monk Cross, which you don't. Court Farm has been connected with Tom Faggus, a highwayman in Blackmore's 'Lorna Doone'.

Along the road for a short distance and you come to the bridge. Just beyond are the stables for one of the last three remaining packs of staghounds in England. There is a smithy here too. The river crossing has a long pedigree. It can be traced back to the Bronze Age and was originally part of the ancient Harepath trackway which linked the Midlands with Cornwall. Up until 1930, a wooden packhorse bridge spanned the river. The present stone-built version, while not so quaint, is attractive to the eye nonetheless.

And so into Exford (which should be pronounced Ex-ford), just opposite the White Horse. What better entry point. . .

WALK 8: MINEHEAD

Route: Bratton, Wydon Farm, Burgundy Chapel, Greenaleigh Farm, Culver Cliff Wood, Minehead Harbour, Higher Town, Woodcombe, Higher Woodcombe

Distance: 6 miles

Map: Ordnance Survey Pathfinder 1215 (SS 84/94)

Start: Bratton Court, Pathfinder map reference 946463

How to get there: No chance of your missing Minehead, self-proclaimed gateway to Exmoor. All roads lead there (not least the A39 which passes its front door), or so it sometimes seems. That is because this town has become the seaside resort of Somerset, complete with holiday camp. Bright and breezy it may be in places but fortunately the Blackpool-of-the-Bristol-Channel it isn't, as this walk demonstrates.

The Pubs

Not surprisingly, there are more to choose from in Minehead than in any other part of the national park. I opted for two, very different in character but attractive in their individual ways.

You will probably come to the first driving into the town if approaching from the east. **The Kildare Lodge** in Townsend Road (tel: 0643 702009) is more inn than bar; a large building which lays back from the road in a residential area towards the outskirts of the town. Small, cosy and intimate it isn't. But the facilities are first class, much of it having been recently rebuilt or refurbished; the welcome is warm; and the choice of real ales is wide and varied. Take your pick from Ushers Best Bitter, Ruddles County, Websters Yorkshire Best Bitter and Cotleigh Tawny Bitter. Oh yes, and don't forget Symonds' Scrumpy Jack if you fancy supping cider instead. It's all there, on hand pump.

The Kildare caters for most needs: the hungry; the peckish; devotees of cream teas; vegetarians; children; lovers of garden bars; but most of all, of course, the plain, downright thirsty. There is plenty of room to spread yourself too. It may be large but this inn began life in 1907 as a private residence and, although much changed, it still has the welcoming atmosphere that you expect in someone's home.

Agreeable but in a totally different way is the **Old Ship Aground** (tel: 064370 2087), backing onto the harbour and alongside the lifeboat station. Cosy and intimate are appropriate terms in this case. It has a comfortable, well-worn feeling, a bit like putting on a pair of familiar old slippers. You get the impression that the atmospheric fishermen's bar really is popular with the local fishermen. Certainly there is no shortage of marine memorabilia.

This old watering hole used to be called The Pier, apparently. Its patio, usually open only in the summer, is popular with families and a good spot from which to watch the boating world go by. As you do, quaff a jar or two of real ale. Ruddles County and Courage Best Bitter are both

Seagull's-eye-view of Minehead.

on hand pump in the two bars here. Lunchtimes and evenings, you can get appetising snacks and meals too, including vegetarian options. How about crispy coated courgettes or crumb-coated Brie wedges? Mmm, tasty.

The Walk

There is plenty of parking in Minehead, not least on the promenade near the harbour. But having dropped into the Kildare Lodge, I opted to start my walk outside the town, at Bratton, so that the Old Ship Aground became a resting place approximately half way round.

The hamlet of Bratton has a claim to fame in the form of Bratton Court. This 15th century manor house is said to have been the birthplace of judge and jurist Henry de Bracton. You can search your memory for his name as you follow the farm track up towards Bratton Ball. There are no signposts or waymarks but the route is clearly defined here.

Once through a gate and into a field, hug the hedgerow to your left rather than following the pecks indicating the right of way on the Ordnance Survey map which run along the top edge of the field. That is because at Wydon Farm the footpath has been diverted around the western side of buildings here via a permissive path. Watch out for foxes around Bratton Ball: according to the locals, they are relatively tame because of the few people seen here. There were plenty of blackberries and mushrooms when I passed through.

Beyond the farm, you pick up red waymarks on a track heading uphill. But pause a while here and look back the way you have come. Spread out before you is a patchwork quilt of fields, all reds and greens and dotted with cows. Beyond can be seen the rooftops of Minehead spread out as if at your disposal. Notice the high proportion of red sandstone buildings, a peculiarity of the area. Further on still can clearly be seen Blue Anchor Bay and the open sea.

Uphill again and you reach what is literally the high point of this walk. Just beyond some cattle grids and after crossing a narrow road is a spot height: you are 257m above sea level says the map. This is North Hill, a popular viewpoint. To the west can clearly be seen Selworthy Beacon while south westwards lies Exmoor's highest point of all, Dunkery Beacon.

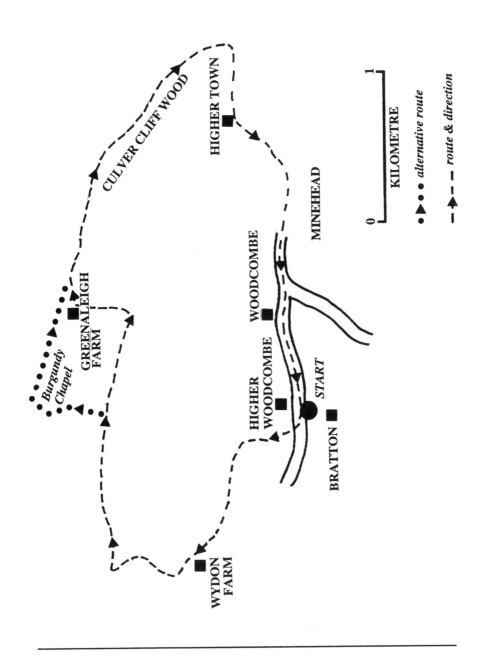

It's downhill all the way to Minehead from here. But you are not there yet. . .

Head seawards. The land drops away steeply below North Hill; just how steeply you will find out shortly. Signposts and waymarks abound from now on. The reason: this is the Somerset & North Devon Coast Path which runs the length of the south west peninsula, joining up with other national trails in Cornwall, South Devon and Dorset to link Minehead with Poole, 515 footpath miles away.

The area here is a sea of gorse dotted with tumuli, cairns and other signs of prehistoric man. Look in particular for Furzebury Brake over to the north west, the site of an ancient settlement discernible on the 236m hill top which doubles as a spot height.

Follow the signs eastwards towards Minehead. To the north Grexy and Bramble provide two clearly defined examples of the wooded combes which are such a characteristic feature of Exmoor. On a sunny day, the seascape is magnificent, with the coast of Wales clearly visible across the Bristol Channel to the north. Even on a dull, damp day the broad expanse of mauve heather and yellow gorse covering the moorland, acres and acres of the stuff, excites and impresses. Regardless of how overcast the weather, the moor here can be a mass of colour, all different shades of purple, fuschia, yellow, pink and green; so many, it is impossible to count. A northward loop from the main Minehead path provides an extra opportunity to drink your fill of the seascape.

Soon you find yourself back alongside that narrow road crossed earlier which runs along the top of the ridge. Stay on the seaward side and follow the signs to Burgundy Chapel. It lies at the foot of the combe of the same name and the descent is steep, the narrow footpath winding its way down the hill, down, down, down. No one knows the origins of the name. Possibly Burgundy Chapel was a hermitage. Or a tomb. It dates back into the mists of time. Ponder its past history as you prepare yourself for the return journey back up to the ridge-top path.

That's the most rewarding route back into Minehead, with seagulls'-eye-views along the way to keep you on your toes. But you don't have to take it. The easier, if less spectacular, option is to stay at foreshore level and follow the foot of the cliffs eastwards past Greenaleigh Sand and Greenaleigh Point.

I took the high road. It was worth the effort, even if only for the surrealistic first view of Greenaleigh beach down through the trees far below me: black sand and white surf. Shortly I headed back down through those trees, down the steep hillside to Greenaleigh Farm where the footpath becomes a farm track. The fields which form the farm look on the map like an enormous pimple stuck onto the coastline as an afterthought. It is surrounded on three sides by sea and sand; with the fourth side being the northernmost flank of North Hill. Only from the eastern side of Minehead do you realise just how dramatically North Hill dominates the town. The Hill is in fact the first in a series of spectacular hog's-backed cliffs running virtually uninterruptedly along the coastline westwards the width of Exmoor all the way to Combe Martin in North Devon.

Following the wide, clearly defined track, you leave behind Greenaleigh, which is National Trust property, and pass through Culver Cliff Wood, bearing left where the route forks and all the time gently descending. Until all of a sudden you are out of the trees, at the foot of the hill and on the promenade, strolling into Minehead alongside its two-mile-long partly sand but mainly pebble beach. Up ahead the Old Ship Aground comes into view.

This is the quieter corner of Minehead which, even at its brashest, is one of the more genteel of seaside resorts. If you get the chance, ask one of the locals about a local legend, the whistling ghost of Mistress Leakey . . .

The harbour, next to the Old Ship, was described by Daniel Defoe in the 1720s as 'fairer, and much deeper, than those at Watchet and Porlock.' Judge for yourself. Your route, beyond pub and harbour, takes you along Quay Street for a short distance before you turn inland, passing through a line of old fishermen's cottages on the seafront near a signpost pointing the way to North Hill ('Combe Martin 35 miles'). Of more significance perhaps is another sign marking the start of the South West Peninsula Coast Path. (Next stop, Poole in Dorset, 515 footsore miles away..?) Follow Church Path and Church Steps up as far as the church itself, a handsome, medieval building noted for Perpendicular tower, Jacobean pulpit and 15th century brasses.

You are now in the heart of Higher Town, full of steep streets and cobbled alleys with quaint old names like The Ball lined with attractive old houses. A place to wander and wonder.

When you have, head down Vicarage Road, opposite the church, to White Cross. There you join, but thankfully for only a few hundred yards, the original A39 before branching off right at Woodcombe and following the lane back to your starting point near Bratton Court.

Looking seawards past Bratton Court and over the rooftops of Minehead.

WALK 9: BRENDON HILL

Route: Ralegh's Cross, Tripp Barrow, Stolford Wood, Roborough Gate Radio Station, Sminhays Corner, Brendon Hill

Distance: 5 miles

Map: Ordnance Survey Pathfinder 1236 (ST 03/13)

Start: Ralegh's Cross Inn, Pathfinder map reference 038344

How to get there: Brendon Hill is one of the access points into Exmoor, on its south eastern edge and the meeting point of the B3224 and B3190. The surrounding area is known as the Brendon Hills.

The Pub

Ralegh's Cross: no, the spelling is not a mistake. The Inn of the same name (tel: 0984 40343) stands near the site of a medieval cross which served as a landmark on the Brendon Ridgeway and was named after the Ralegh family of nearby Nettlecombe Court.

It's an isolated spot, high up, with views across to the Welsh coast on a clear day. The pub is just about the only building of any size around here, large, white painted and set well back from the road. You have plenty of space to spread yourself, both indoors and out. No shortage of parking here, nor of garden space, complete with picnic tables a-plenty: there's even an assault course playground for the children. That's not to mention a replica of a medieval beacon brazier, the type used to give warning of the Spanish Armada. The reason for its presence is because Elworthy, just along the road, was one of the original beacon sites.

Children are catered for inside as well, where there is a family room. Nor have non-smokers been forgotten. Morning coffee and cream teas are served as well as snacks, lunches, evening meals and real ales. You could choose between a special, Whitbread's Ralegh Cross Inn Bitter, and Flowers Original Bitter or Exmoor Ale when I visited. There was draught Symonds' Scrumpy Jack served by handpump too.

Focal point of the single, lengthy bar is a well, now glassed over, which must be 25ft deep. Maybe someone will count all the coins in the water down below one day. . .

You can see where the original building has been extended even though the developers made a concerted effort to match the original wooden beamed ceiling. Two large stone fireplaces with wood burning stoves should keep things nice'n'cosy in the winter. In the summer whippet races have sometimes been held. And of course there is accommodation should you require it.

There are the inevitable hunt trophies. But most of the memorabilia strung across the extensive walls tells the fascinating story of the time when iron ore was mined in them there Brendon Hills. More of that as you follow the walk. . .

Exmoor ponies – short in stature; long, hairy overcoats and infinitely appealing

The Walk

This is a route which offers some names to conjure with: how about Huish Champflower? Or Robbery Gate and its obviously bastardised neighbour, Roborough Gate Farm? And how did Naked Boy's Bridge and the adjacent Naked Boy's Stone come to be so named? We may guess or speculate but I suspect that we shall never know for sure.

You can ponder such thoughts as you follow the blue waymarks from the signpost which marks the start of the walk and points you due southwards towards Tripp Farm. Following a tumulus you pass a barrow of the same name, one of many ancient settlements which are dotted about the area. Shortly, you top the crest of the hill alongside the barrow and touch 370m above sea level; by Exmoor standards, a high point on the moor. Except that this isn't moorland. The Brendon Hills may be within the national park and form part of Exmoor but they are very different in character to the hinterland to the west, gentler, kinder, more pastoral. It's an altogether more agricultural, farming outlook here.

As you descend towards Tripp Farm, Clatworthy Reservoir comes into clear view straight ahead. It is one of the largest bodies of water in the area and, with its picnic sites, viewpoints and nature trails, a popular family leisure centre. But our route takes us away to the west, down into a combe where the River Tone, which feeds Clatworthy, runs through Stolford Wood.

The going is muddy in places here and, despite the occasional blue waymark, not always crystal clear on the ground. Which, when visibility allows, makes the masts of the radio station straight ahead near Robbery Gate all the more useful as a navigation beacon. Long before that, the footpath becomes, first, a bridle path, then a sunken lane before bisecting the metalled lane linking the Beverton and Brown – Lower, Middle and Higher – Farms. (One hopes, if only for the postman's sake, that there isn't a Farmer Brown resident at all three. . .)

At that metalled lane you can if you wish cut short the route, by half in fact, and return to Ralegh's Cross via Lower Beverton Bridge. Otherwise continue westwards across the fields, climbing gently all the way until you reach another high point, marked on the map as a spot height of 404m alongside those radio station masts.

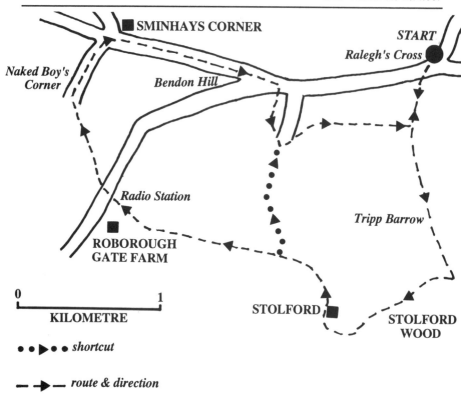

SMINHAYS CORNER

START
Ralegh's Cross

Naked Boy's
Corner

Bendon Hill

Radio Station

Tripp Barrow

ROBOROUGH
GATE FARM

0   1

KILOMETRE

STOLFORD

STOLFORD
WOOD

● ● ▶ ● ● *shortcut*

— ➔ — *route & direction*

Just down the road as you contemplate the homeward leg back to the
Inn is Beverton Pond, where the Tone river rises. But first, cut across the
fields, downhill now and north westwards, to Naked Boy's Bridge with,
beyond it, Naked Boy's Stone. Sure enough there is a $3^1/_2$ft standing
stone among the grass at the roadside.

Having walked from the bridge to the stone you have crossed the route
of the old Mineral Line. The West Somerset Mineral Railway, to give its
full name, dates back to the latter half of the 19th century. It may be
hard to imagine now, given the peaceful rural setting, but in those days
this was the heart of an industrial complex.

Iron ore was extracted from these hills by the Romans. In the
Elizabethan age, German miners were brought in especially to dig the
ore. But it was as recently as 1877 that mining for iron reached its peak.

Moorland Memorial to a World War 2 soldier.

The quantities and logistical problems involved were so great that the Victorians developed new technology to cope with them. Witness the mile-long, one-in-four incline which they blasted, dug and shovelled in order to conquer the 1,200ft drop between the minehead near Brendon Hill and the port at Watchet just eight miles to the north. Ralegh's Cross Station preceded the waggons' 800ft descent through Eastern Wood to the Washford river valley below. The railway, an aerial ropeway and the intricate system of pulleys, 18ft drum and winding gear may have gone but the incline where they operated will still be visible for decades, perhaps even centuries, to come.

You will be able to see the line of that incline as you make your way eastwards along the road between Sminhays Corner and Sea View House. That last is well named. For proof, if you haven't already'spotted it, take a look northwards: the Bristol Channel, weather permitting, will be clearly visible. Watchet too, where all those ships laden with Brendon iron ore bound for the smelters of South Wales used to ply their trade.

Notice another signpost as you go: it points the way back to Raleigh's Cross – but with a different spelling to that on the map and the inn sign.

At the junction of the two B roads is another memento and memorial to all those miners: the Beulah Bible Christian (Methodist) Chapel, c.1861. It's uncharacteristic of Exmoor, reflecting more the style of the Cornish miners who worked here between 1853 and 1878. It was in 1878 that the mines, now uneconomic, closed down virtually overnight, a victim of cheap Spanish iron. They may have gone but the chapel is still in use even today.

So too is the pub they used. The village built for the miners at Brendon Hill, itself long gone, did not have an inn of its own. It reflected the views of the Methodist owners of the mines: temperance was next to Godliness. So the thirsty miners had to walk to get a drink – to Ralegh's Cross. Just as you will now. . .

WALK 10: MONKSILVER

Route: Woodford, Monksilver, Birchanger Lane, Birchanger Cross, Pooke Wood, Colton Cross, Bird's Hill, The Old Rectory, Monksilver, Woodford

Distance: 5 miles

Map: Ordnance Survey Pathfinder 1236 (ST 03/13)

Start: Woodford Cemetery, Pathfinder map reference 062384

How to get there: the hamlet of Woodford, near Monksilver, lies almost at the easternmost tip of Exmoor, on the B3188 and straddling the boundary of the national park. The nearest town is Williton, at the junction of the A39 and A358, two miles as the crow flies to the north east.

The Pub

If the good food and good pub guides are to be believed, the social life of Monksilver and satellite settlements such as Woodford revolves around the **Notley Arms** (tel: 0984 56217). Pay a visit or three and you will become a believer. Not that the Notley, named after a local landowning family, has always been known by that name. According to a local historian, it has variously been called the Ram, the Rising Sun, possibly even the Risen Moon during its chequered history.

Be that as it may, this is an attractive village pub in an attractive village setting, all thatched cottages with roses round the front door. And you can be sure of a warm and friendly welcome from the landlord. That applies whether you are a visiting walker or a local regular.

There are all the usual facilities of a well organised hostelry: plenty of car parking, a family room (complete with toys, which is not so usual); assorted mementoes and memorabilia on the walls (including a goodly collection of old master prints but, uncommonly for Exmoor, no hunt

Combe Sydenham – a fine Elizabethan manor house familiar to Francis Drake

trophies); and a pleasant garden complete with tables, even its own stream. Honest-to-goodness wooden tables, candle-lit on dark evenings; small settles and kitchen chairs furnish the single, L-shaped, bar. Timbered walls, an oak beamed ceiling and wood-burning stoves add to the cosiness. There is even a skittle alley. You will immediately feel at home here.

And that's even before you quench your thirst or indulge a good appetite. Real ales, all on handpump at the Arms, include Theakstons Best, Usher's Best, Wadworth 6X and Ruddles County, plus a selection of ciders. You can sample some Somerset country wines too: how about a glass of oak leaf or raspberry?

While you are about it, don't overlook the blackboard menu, lunchtimes and evenings, for which the Notley has won awards. Richman's Purse, full of garlic beef, and Poor Man's Pouch, with a filling of cheese, are just two of the imaginative Pitta bread snacks on offer. For something more substantial try the Chinese style, red-roast-pork stir fry followed by treacle tart. And it isn't only vegetarians who will appreciate the aubergine and butterbean Biriani.

After all that, you will need this walk. . .

The Walk

It isn't monks in whose silver footsteps you walk at Monksilver but those of a national hero. Every schoolboy knows about the exploits of Sir Francis Drake. But few will be able to tell you that he courted his second wife, Elizabeth, here, no doubt enjoying the wooded combes as much as you will.

Our route starts near an old cemetery midway between Nettlecombe and Woodford. Nettlecombe Court, now a field centre, was formerly the home of the Raleigh family, another name with a familiar ring to it. . .

From the lane a signpost with yellow waymarks points the way: next stop, Monksilver. Simply stick to the yellow flashes which follow the course of the stream to your left. A glance at the map shows that a short distance downstream there is a flurry of farms and hamlets, all of which take their names from this little watercourse: Higher Stream, Lower

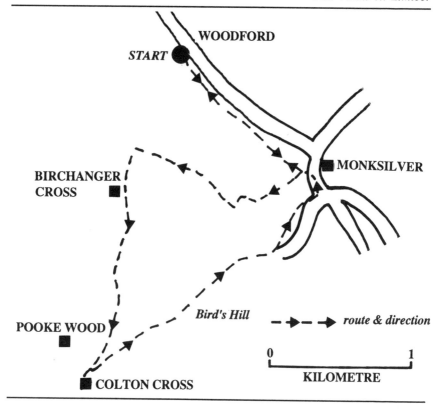

Stream and plain, simple, straightforward Stream. No prizes for originality there.

This rivulet is not named on the Ordnance Survey map but the upper reaches are fed by a watercourse known as, surprise, surprise, Drake's Leat. That isn't the only reminder of his links with the area, as you will discover later.

As you follow the course of the stream south eastwards and make your way across the fields, through woodland and, at one stage, over a footbridge, the Norman tower of Monksilver church comes into clear view ahead. From its sloping churchyard, the church overlooks this pretty little village with its colour-washed cottages. Rose trees line the path leading to its 15th century south door. But you must wait for a closer look till later because for the moment the route heads off south westwards.

From the quaintly named Pond Orchard, a signpost complete with yellow waymark directs you towards Birchanger Lane. Several more lead you across the fields to the Lane, which then takes you around Birchanger Farm and up past Birchanger Cross. Eventually it brings you through the spookily named Pooke Wood to the highest point of the walk, Colton Cross. Here it's time to leave the lane and strike off into the woods for the return leg, north eastwards and still waymarked in yellow.

It's downhill all the way from here back into Monksilver, which is signposted (no excuses for getting lost). The upper reaches of the path were wide and clear cut when I walked it. Well cut too: it looked as if someone had been busy with a giant lawnmower. Further down, the track becomes a sunken lane. Further still, overhanging trees had turned the lane almost into a tunnel: it could be quite gloomy on a dull day.

Nonetheless, whatever the weather, you will enjoy the views as you descend through the trees which cover Bird's Hill. Over to the north west watch out for Nettlecombe. Directly to the north, see if you can spot your starting point down at Woodford. Closer to hand, keep a wary eye open for fallow deer. Descendants of escapers from the deer park at Nettlecombe Court have been seen among the plantations around Monksilver. Off through the trees and continuing the watery theme already encountered on this route is Pond Wood.

Drake must have been familiar with these views. The family he married into, the Sydenhams, lived just over the hill at Combe Sydenham. Their fine Elizabethan manor house, in red sandstone, is a sight worth seeing, although not typical Exmoor in style. It has become a private family home now, part of a 500-acre country park which is open to the public.

Old walled gardens, ornamental tree nurseries, a trout farm and a corn mill with water-wheel are just some of the attractions. That's not to mention ten miles of woodland walks which take in a deserted hamlet. Nor a shop selling home made bread and venison in just about every form you could think of, including venison sausages and venison burgers. The mind boggles. Access to Combe Sydenham, half a mile away, is via the B3188 from Monksilver, which beckons ahead.

Leaving the woods, the footpath crosses a couple of fields before rejoining Birchanger Lane by The Old Rectory. Not for the first time on this walk you are likely to see signs of badger activity in the hedgerows.

Follow the lane down into the village. Now's your chance to quench that thirst at the Notley Arms and renew the inner man. It is also an opportunity to take a closer look at those olde English thatched country cottages with their trailing roses. You can also now explore the church, with its carvings and a gargoyle with what looks like a wicked penchant for dentistry.

Your curiosity and thirst satisfied, head down Pond Orchard again and rejoin the streamside footpath for the return journey, this time heading north westwards, back to the starting point at Woodford. From there, if you want to find out more about Drake and the mysterious legend of the cannonball, it is only a short drive to Combe Sydenham. Another local legend has it that the ghost of Sir George Sydenham rides down Sydenham Combe on certain nights. So if it is already beginning to get dark, perhaps it would be better to delay your visit until another day. . .

Combe Sydenham, one of Francis Drake's old haunts, offers several walks

WALK 11: BRENDON

Route: Brendon, Mill Wood, Rockford, Oaklands, Gratton Lane, Shilstone Farm, Shilstone Hill, Dry Bridge, Cross Gate, Cross Lane, Leeford

Distance: 6 miles

Map: Ordnance Survey Pathfinder 1214 (SS 64/74)

Start: Brendon Bridge, Pathfinder map reference 769482

How to get there: Brendon lies in the north western corner of Exmoor, less than three miles from the coast and four from Lynton. It can be reached by turning south off the A39 down an unclassified road – watch for signs pointing to the village.

The Pub

You are unlikely to stumble across the **Rockford Inn** (tel: 05987 214) by accident, tucked away as it is down a steep, narrow, winding lane going from nowhere especially to nowhere in particular. Which makes it all the pleasanter a find.

Understandably treasuring their secret, locals are only too familiar with the Inn. You can tell that from the clientele and from the fact that this little 'freehouse and tea rooms', as its sign proclaims, dates back to the 17th century.

There are oak beams galore. A clutch of firearms decorates the walls. But don't expect any frills and fripperies: you won't find any. And the Rockford is none the worse for that. On the contrary. It's a cosy, intimate little pub with a well-worn feel and, unusually, the single bar is on two levels. A simple open fire, just like the one that used to be a feature of every living room, provides a domestic touch. The walls are decorated with photographs from long ago, also just like home: friends and relatives, the inn in days gone by, views of the neighbourhood . . . you know the sort of thing.

In fact it's just the sort of place where you might go of a Sunday morning to pass the time of day, catch up on the latest gossip and relax in an armchair while reading the newspaper – which in fact is just what happens.

But don't forget the main reason for the Rockford's existence: quenching the thirst and refreshing the inner man (and woman). They serve a good pint of real ale here. Cotleigh Tawny Bitter, Courage Directors and Courage Best were all available on handpump when I visited; Symonds' Scrumpy Jack too for those with a taste for cider.

And of course there is accommodation and country cooking to go with it, all at the Rockford Inn, nestling in the Doone Valley.

I said it was popular with the locals. The same applies to walkers following the course of the East Lyn river which the Rockford overlooks. You don't need to glance twice at the boulder strewn stream with its ford and footbridge to realise why this rural retreat was located where it is and how it got its name. Quaffing your ale, you'll enjoy the view across the river all the more having stepped out the following walk.

The Walk

Our starting point, Brendon, is one of the original Exmoor settlements. It can trace its roots at least as far back as 1086 when there was a manor recorded here, Brandone; one which developed in due course into the village you see today. It isn't difficult to guess why the original settlers chose their site. Unlike large tracts of Exmoor, this well-wooded and extra wide river valley provided shelter from the upland storms. A far cry in human habitation terms from the bleak open moorland of Brendon Common which lies just a mile or so to the south.

Not much further away, both to east and south, is the Somerset border. Although this is Exmoor still, you are in Devon now, not that you would know from the countryside. It follows much the same pattern here as in the northern reaches of the national park on the Somerset side of the county boundary.

From the old stone road bridge in the centre of Brendon, follow the riverside footpath as it meanders its way westwards along the hillside

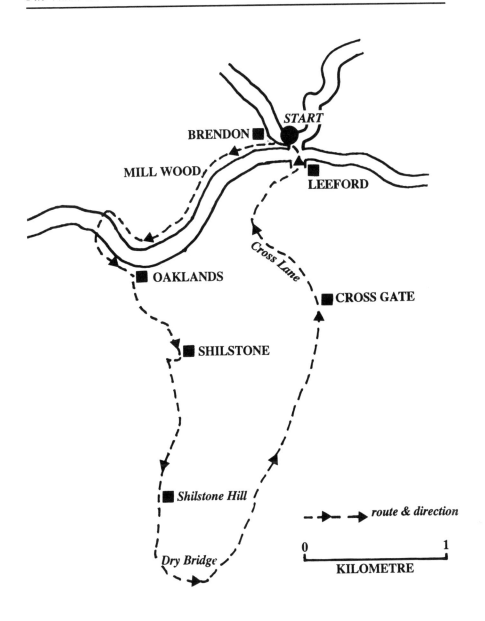

BRENDON

START

MILL WOOD

LEEFORD

Cross Lane

OAKLANDS

CROSS GATE

SHILSTONE

Shilstone Hill

route & direction

0   1

Dry Bridge

KILOMETRE

through Mill Wood. Geese, long horned sheep and Exmoor ponies will all provide company at various stages along the route. There seem to be more footbridges on this river than any other I have come across. Perhaps that simply reflects the small number of road bridges. Whatever, ignore them all until you reach Rockford where you cross just opposite the Inn.

Time for a quick half or three?

Whether you go in or not, our route leads down the lane, back towards Brendon, for a few hundred yards to Oaklands. As a point of interest, were you to head westwards along the lane you would shortly come to St Brendan's parish church. Yes, here, a full mile from the village and beyond Rockford hamlet. For the record it was rebuilt in 1738 then further restored in the 19th century. The pretty sundial over the porch, c.1707, and the Norman font are worth the detour.

Back at Oaklands, by a public footpath sign to Brendon Common, turn right and head uphill through the trees, alongside a small stream. It's quite steep here, a pronounced contrast to the gently undulating woodland path you followed on the other side of the river. But the effort is worthwhile: the steepness of the slope has produced several small waterfalls in the stream you are following back towards its source.

There is an even more marked contrast in surroundings later but we shall come to that in due course. Where the woodland and the climb peter out you join Gratton Lane for a short dogleg before branching off across the gently rising fields which lead to Shilstone. It's beyond the farm here that the surrounding land begins to change dramatically.

As you gain height, slowly but steadily, the nature of the landscape alters totally. Gone are the cultivated fields and the wooded river valley to be replaced by open, treeless moorland covered in bracken and rough grassland. And the higher you go, the more open the landscape and the more marked the contrast becomes. Until eventually you reach the walk's highest point, indicated by a trig point on the crest of Shilstone Hill. At 405m above sea level to be exact.

Here it is almost as if you are touching the sky. To the north the land falls away to the fields and farms which follow the course of the East

Lyn river before rising again briefly at Countisbury Common and then dropping almost sheer into the sea. To the south is the original Exmoor Forest, with barely a tree in sight, the term having originally been used to describe a royal hunting ground. The moor looms large, a plateau which rises only another 50m higher than this trig point over the next dozen miles before it begins to peter away into the mid Devon lowlands.

Brendon Common itself, which is now spread out before you, offers great open stretches of moorland, some of the most impressive and loneliest Exmoor has to offer. This is one of the best areas for heather and ling, interspersed with gorse, bracken and the odd thorn tree. Punctuating the moor are small valleys where streams trickle and the unwary can find themselves paddling in a bog.

A few miles to the south west is eerie Pinkworthy (pronounced Pinkery) Pond and The Chains, a notoriously misty and boggy area with a fearsome reputation locally.

Our route heads down to Dry Bridge before swinging round Shilstone Hill and back across Brendon Common towards Tippacott Ridge. As you leave the bridge, a cairn comes into view topped by a star. It is a crude yet moving memorial to a soldier killed during World War 2.

A detour eastwards via Lankcombe Ford and signposted Doone Valley will take you to Badgworthy (pronounced Badgery) Water. There you can follow in the ghostly footsteps of R. D. Blackmore's Lorna Doone and Jon Ridd; even visit the church at Oare immortalised by the novelist.

Otherwise, it's homeward, or at least Brendon bound, downhill off the Common and back among the fields and hedgerows again. And as you descend, the village comes into full view, its buildings scattered along the wooded valley sides with the high moor surrounding it virtually on all sides. The name, appropriately enough, means 'broom hill' but has nothing to do with Brendon Hill ('brown hill') across the Somerset border on the eastern edge of Exmoor. It provides yet one more contrast on a walk which has been punctuated by them.

WALKS 12 & 13: COUNTISBURY

Route 1: Countisbury, Wind Hill, Wester Wood, Myrtleberry Cleave, Watersmeet, Barton Wood, Ash Bridge, Horner's Neck Wood, South Hill Common

Route 2: Countisbury, Butter Hill, Great Red, The Foreland, Coddow Combe, Foreland Point, Barna Barrow, Countisbury

Distance: *route 1*, 6 miles; *route 2*, 4 miles (or, with linking section, about 11 miles combined; or short cuts reduce routes if required.)

Map: Ordnance Survey Pathfinder 1214 (SS 64/74)

Start: all routes, car park opposite Exmoor Sandpiper Inn, Pathfinder map reference 496747

How to get there: you cannot miss Countisbury, right on the A39, at the top of the infamous Countisbury Hill, on the northern edge of Exmoor and a couple of miles east of Lynton.

The Pub

A rose by any other name? This hostelry has certainly had its share of handles. Currently the **Exmoor Sandpiper Inn** (tel: 05987 263), it apparently started life as the Blue Bore c.1800 and became briefly in 1986 (for less than two years would you believe) the Blue Ball. It's that last name which adorns the road junction sign here. But it's a wild boar which features in an ornate stained glass panel over the main bar. There are four oak beamed bars in all, reflecting the rambling size of this inn.

Outside and in, the white washed building looks like a collection of cottages which have been pushed together then fixed there. Parts of it date back to the 15th century, some to the 13th. Notice the unusual chimney, tall, round and heavily cowled.

Watersmeet – where the East Lyn and Hoar Oak Water come together

As recently as 1913 the inn was a stopping place for the horse-drawn coach which plied between Lynmouth and Minehead. There are photographs on the wall to prove it. Travellers then would have appreciated its hospitality just as they do today, whether staying for one night or one week, for a meal (the menu includes local venison) or simply to quench the thirst with a draught of real ale. On offer to do that when I called were Marston's Pedigree Bitter, Exmoor Ale and Symonds' Scrumpy Jack cider, all on handpump.

There is room to spread yourself at the Sandpiper: it just seems to go on and on. Which means somewhere for the family and somewhere to eat and somewhere to enjoy pub games (pool, darts) as well as somewhere to enjoy a jar or two. Favourite are the inglenook fireplaces. Those, like the horse brasses, hunt trophies and old advertising signs are not unusual in a drinking house. But a collection of old electric kettles?! Who would have thought tea making equipment could be so fascinating.

Blackpool Bridge over the East Lyn – designed to float away . . .

The Walks

This is National Trust territory, an area criss-crossed by so many footpaths through attractive and contrasting scenery that one walk could not even begin to do it justice. So here are two. Using the Sandpiper as a starting point, you can choose between longer and shorter routes or, alternatively, combine them to form one large figure of eight route. You could even pick'n'choose from the two to produce a short'n'simple stroll of a couple of miles or so. The choice is yours.

Walk 1: this is well signposted and waymarked throughout, and wanders the 2,000-acre Watersmeet estate. It's as pretty and dramatic a setting as you could wish for with its fast flowing rivers and steep wooded hillsides. Be prepared to exert yourself: it's well worth the effort.

It starts off with a breathtaking view; the charmingly named Myrtleberry Cleave framed by the bulk of Wind Hill (261m) and South Hill Common (287m). Initially the footpath maintains its height, skirting Countisbury Camp on Wind Hill. This Iron Age promontory fort has ramparts 11m wide and 3.5m high. It was the site of the battle of Cynwit, fought between the Saxons and invading Vikings in AD 877-8.

That brings you into the Watersmeet oak woods, a prolific breeding ground for birds and a Site of Special Scientific Interest. Below you through the trees, ash, elm and alder as well as oak, you will catch site of the oddly named Arnold's Lindhay. But more of that later.

So on through Wester Wood where you can see the rare Vexans Whitebeam tree of which there are only about 30 specimens world-wide. Count the lichens here, if you can, and the total will come to 52 apparently. The high number is a sign of the low level of air pollution. Breathe deeply.

Shortly you turn left, south west, down a long flight of wooden steps through the trees known as Sparrow's Walk after the benefactor responsible. Those bring you to the edge of the East Lyn river. On the opposite bank can be seen the remnants of a miniature canal. They are all that remain of one of the very first hydro-electric plants to be established in Britain. It kept the lights on in Lynton and Lynmouth

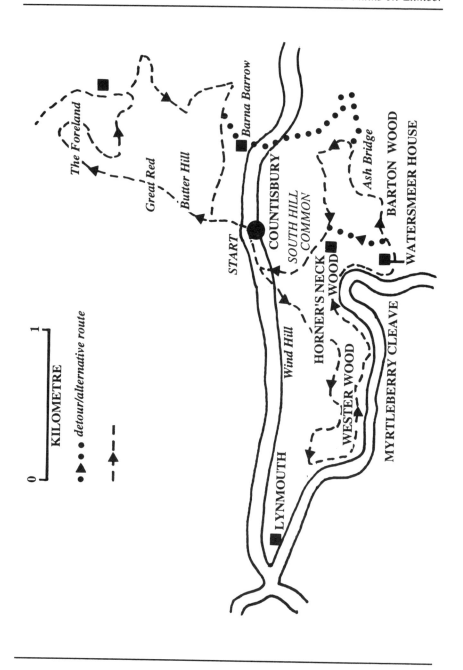

●▲● ● *detour/alternative route*

The Foreland

Great Red

Butter Hill

Barna Barrow

COUNTISBURY

START

Wind Hill

SOUTH HILL COMMON

HORNER'S NECK WOOD

WESTER WOOD

LYNMOUTH

MYRTLEBERRY CLEAVE

Ash Bridge

BARTON WOOD

WATERSMEER HOUSE

from the early 1900s right up until the flood disaster in 1952.

Follow the course of the river south east, upstream as far as a footbridge. Cross here: this is Blackpool Bridge, one of several which had to be built following the wholesale destruction caused by the Lynmouth flood disaster in 1952. The bridges now are designed to float away under such fierce flood conditions rather than, as then, forming artificial dams which caused mayhem when they eventually collapsed under the weight of water and accumulated flotsam.

A short distance upstream, glance across to the opposite bank. The hillside is made up of a flight of ten stone walls forming a series of terraces. This is Arnold's Lindhay, mentioned earlier. It dates back to the 18th century and has variously been described as an area for growing crops and enclosures where a local trader called Arnold kept packhorses.

Continuing on, you come to an old stone wall with a bottle set into it. Back in the early 1900s this was the site of the Lyn Rock Mineral Factory where local spring water was bottled. Eat your heart out Perrier.

The next port of call, after passing Myrtleberry North Camp, the site of another ancient fort, is pretty Watersmeet. No prizes for guessing that it lies at the meeting place of two rivers, the East Lyn and Hoar Oak Water. Make a short detour up the Hoar Oak to bag a brace of waterfalls. At one of the several leaps, you may spot a salmon or trout making its way the 15 miles up-river, climbing 1500ft in the process, to lay its eggs up on the moor at the river's source.

Watersmeet House was built about 1830 by the Halliday family as a fishing and shooting lodge. Lucky old Hallidays: what a place to spend your holidays. Now it's a National Trust shop and restaurant. Don't miss (you couldn't anyway) the huge Monterey pine growing on the garden lawn. A sight to behold, like so much along this walk.

From here it is possible to take a short cut through Horner Neck Wood back to the starting point beyond South Hill Common. Otherwise, continuing up-river, the footpath passes an old but restored lime kiln with, in among the trees nearby, a miniature quarry where the stone used to build Watersmeet House was extracted. Many of the paths on the estate had their origins as mule or donkey tracks used in the 18th and 19th centuries to run the charcoal and tanning industries which were widespread in the area.

This is Barton Wood, boasting even more different types of tree, including larch and beech planted nearly 50 years ago.

So you come to Ash Bridge where the final leg of this walk kicks off. It is time to regain all that height sacrificed at Sparrow's Steps only this time the ascent is more gradual, the path edging its way up the hillside, climbing as it goes and passing through the various woods: Scrip, Tilly and finally Horner's Neck. Only by this time you are above the tree line and soon come to Winstone's Path, out in the open with panoramic views again across and down Myrtleberry Cleave. It's as dramatic a finish as was the start: breathtaking and beautiful.

Walk 2

Glance at any map of North Devon and you will notice a blip or pimple sticking out on the coastline midway between Ilfracombe and Minehead. That is Foreland Point. It is to the lighthouse at the tip of the Point that this second walk leads.

The starting point is the same as for the first walk: the car park opposite the Exmoor Sandpiper Inn alias the Blue Ball/Boar. Ball incidentally is a local term for hill: very appropriate given the proximity of Countisbury Hill. Back in 1899 the Lynmouth lifeboat was dragged the 1,000ft up the steep gradient and past this spot purely by man power. It needed to go to the assistance of a ship in distress but could not be launched because of the roughness of the sea. The crew finally got afloat after an 11-hour haul to Porlock Weir, nearly seven miles away as the crow flies. The ship's crew were saved.

Walk up the lane past St John's church. The small cottage just outside the church yard used to be the local school. With a population of just 60, Countisbury no longer has its own.

Here you join the Somerset & North Devon Coast Path. The crest of Butter Hill (302m), the high point ahead, is your target. At the top is a long disused signal station, now adapted to serve as a television booster station. The residents of Lynton and Lynmouth depend upon it to watch the latest episodes of Coronation Street and Neighbours. You will be able to see South Wales directly to the north from here (not on a tv!) if the weather is kind. The island far out to sea to the west is Lundy, nearly 40 miles away.

Look just ahead downhill: the gaping landslip is called Great Red. For geology lovers, that is where the Lynton slates meet the Foreland grits. The route passes the edge but keep away as the cliff is unstable.

Continue on, with care, to the top of The Foreland. From this point the Devon and Somerset coastline stretches away to east and west seemingly forever. It truly is a grandstand view from the tip of this bold, bare, sheep-grazed yet majestic headland.

The lighthouse lies at the foot of Foreland Point but don't be tempted to try and scramble down the cliff face. Circle back round almost back to Great Red until you pick up the signpost and waymark (there are plenty of those along the route) pointing the way. That will take you down a clearly defined footpath into the arid, steep sided cleft known as Coddow Combe with its acres of scree-covered slopes.

Notice the contrast with the grassy mounds, like huge turtle shells, which make up the earlier part of The Foreland. Notice too the contrast between the fresh green of the grass on those mounds, the dry greyness of the scree and the brown bracken covering the nearby moorland. Finally notice how quiet it is. The National Trust say that this section of the Exmoor coastline is one of the quietest parts of the West Country. I can believe that: even bird song was conspicuous by its absence when I walked this way.

A road gives access to the lighthouse, which is usually open to visitors in the afternoon. In any case you will find the spot a rewarding observation point for sea birds: gannets can sometimes be seen diving for fish off the headland.

Retrace your steps, by-passing the oddly named Warmersturt – that's the rocky hill opposite the point at which you joined the lighthouse road earlier. Continue on up the road. You will see little traffic because although open to walkers it's otherwise private. After a series of hairpin bends, you and the road part company, just below the crest of Barna

Barrow (323m). Heading westwards brings you back to the church at Countisbury and so to your starting point.

To link up with the first walk, instead of heading westwards for half a mile circle round Barna Barrow in an anti-clockwise direction until you reach the road. Careful: this is the A39. Cut across and follow the right of way downhill past Holden Head. This is known as the Church Path and leads to the hamlet of Wilsham. There were several Exmoor ponies here when I passed by. That brings you into a combe which links up with the other walk at Ash Bridge in Scrip Wood.

Alternatively, from the Exmoor Sandpiper Inn follow the clearly defined footpath through Trilly down to Winstone's Path above Horner's Neck Wood. Taking the Path north westwards provides a very short, circular but scenically stunning walk in its own right.

WALK 14: DULVERTON

Route: Dulverton, Burridge Wood, Earmarsh Pool, Kennel Farm, Marsh Bridge, Looseall Wood, Court Down, Hollam Cross, Hollam, Dulverton

Distance: $4^1/_2$ miles with options of shorter $2^1/_4$ mile route and mile-long circular tour of the town

Map: Ordnance Survey Pathfinder 1256 (SS 82/92)

Start: car park between bridge and National Park Centre, Pathfinder map reference 912278

How to get there: Dulverton lies on the central southern edge of Exmoor, a mile west of the A396 Tiverton to Minehead road and reached via the B3222. It is well signposted.

The Pubs

You have a choice between two markedly different drinking houses in Dulverton, both with their own character and appeal.

The Lion (tel: 0398 23444), which describes itself as the only hotel in Dulverton, is in Bank Square, right at the centre of town. Spick'n'span in its coat of white stone paint, it was recently refurbished and redecorated.

It is the type of pub, with an international atmosphere, which attracts tourists and does a good job at looking after them. So there are beamed ceilings, hunt trophies on the wall, horse brasses, framed photographs, paintings, chintzy upholstery, cosy corners in the bar, discreet lighting. All very intimate. Accommodation is available if you need it, with all the facilities you would expect from an AA two-star hotel with Le Routier recommendation.

You can get a good pint of Exmoor Ale or Ushers Best Bitter, served by handpump. Children are catered for and the welcome is friendly. Both bar and restaurant meals are served, the latter's speciality being a four-course table d'hote menu based on home cooking and local produce.

When 'time' is called in the bar, watch out for the 'bell'. It started life as part of an engine on the ill-fated R101 airship and came to its present home courtesy a former landlord with the unlikely name of Captain Popkiss.

Head down the High Street towards the river and just before the bridge you will come to **The Bridge** (tel: 0398 23694). You couldn't ask for a greater contrast. Here, you have a genuine working man's local. And it's local working men you will find at the bar of the Bridge Inn.

There are few hunt trophies and no frills in the single bar. But you can enjoy a meal and wash it down with a pint of real ale, draught Ushers Best Bitter or traditional Taunton Cider, both on handpump. And the cost will be less than you might expect.

On warm, sunny days you could sit on the riverbank alongside and watch the fishermen – Dulverton is a renowned fly fishing centre. As you do, recall that during the 1952 Lynmouth flood disaster, the Bridge Inn had water up to its ceiling. Perhaps it's time for. . .

Next to The Bridge in Dulverton is . . . the bridge

The Walk

The Barle river valley has been described as the finest introduction to Exmoor that could be wished for. It is upstream, through the thickly wooded valley, that the first leg of this walk meanders.

Cross the river via the medieval road bridge with its five arches. Two inscriptions read: 'Dulverton Bridge: repaired in Ye Year of Our Lord God 1684' and 'Widened 1819 by John Stone'. Leaving Mr Stone's handiwork behind, follow signs, with yellow waymarks, for Beech Tree Cross, Hawkridge and Tarr Steps. The cottages here are the stuff of which retirement dreams are made.

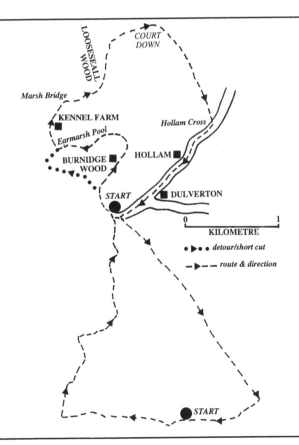

Soon you leave the lane behind and are into Burridge Wood, a designated Site of Special Scientific Interest. That's no wonder considering the flora and fauna to be found here. Watch out for the early purple orchid, wood sorrel, enchanter's nightshade, wood anemone, dog's mercury, bluebells, speckled wood and hairstreak butterflies, spotted flycatchers, wrens, redwings and robins. That's not to mention the mosses and lichens, nor the variety of trees: sessile oak, hazel, birch, ash, beech, holly, hazel and alder.

The area around Earmarsh Pool can get muddy, especially where the footpath crosses a feeder stream trickling its way down to the Barle. Keep alert for signs of red deer.

Here you can if you wish make a detour or cut short the walk. A trail swings off to the south, circling round in an anti-clockwise direction to reach the remains of Oldberry Castle. It was probably built around 400-300BC to deter attacks from neighbouring clans. The castle would originally have stood clear of the woodland, the surrounding fields being used to grow cereal crops and graze domestic animals. Continuing on from the castle in a south easterly direction shortly brings you back to Dulverton again.

Reverting to the original route, you leave the woodland behind after about a mile's riverside walk through Burridge Wood and cross the Barle at Marsh Bridge. It is difficult to imagine, up here in north west Somerset, that the waters of the Barle will end up in the English Channel many miles to the south. Yet that is the case. Because despite the closeness of the north coast and the Bristol Channel, you are south of the watershed. From here to the Devon Riviera, it's downhill all the way.

Our route is in fact now steeply uphill, through Looseall Wood (make sure you don't lose anything. . .). Ignore signs for Hawkridge and Tarr Steps and head instead for Court Down. The bridleway is firm, wide and clearly defined.

Eventually you emerge from the trees onto the down. Make your way uphill and across the fields to the trig point on the crest. From this eagle's eyrie, 316m above sea level, the resulting view will prove to you that the effort earlier was well worthwhile. Within the 360-degree panorama you can pick out (on a clear day) various well known landmarks including Anstey Common, Winsford Hill, Dunkery Beacon, even the edge of Dartmoor, well to the south.

It's all downhill from here, following the yellow waymarks through some rather decimated woodland and across the fields until you join a lane at Hollam Cross. Don't bother diverting northwards to visit the ruins of an Augustinian Priory at Barlynch Farm: although you may catch a glimpse, they are not open to the public. Don't be tempted either to bag any of the pheasants besporting themselves along the sunken lane leading back down into Dulverton. You can look but you mustn't touch.

And so back into the network of little streets and squares that is Dulverton via the oddly named Town Marsh and Jury Road. En route to the car park, you pass the Lion Hotel. . .

Back at your starting point, now is the time, if you didn't before, to pay a visit to Exmoor House, visitor centre and headquarters of the national park. No shortage of information about Exmoor in there. You can't miss it: the park HQ is the classical looking building with the elegant louvred wooden lantern on top next door to the car park. It used to be the workhouse in Victorian times.

Here is also an ideal starting point for a tour of Dulverton.

Although, with its population of just 1,288, more of a large village than a town, it well deserves one. Dolvertune, as it used to be called, was named in the Domesday Book so it has a long pedigree. The name means 'village at the hidden ford': the briefest glance at a map shows why.

Water power has played a large part in its history, as wandering through this small, sleepy town demonstrates. You will cross the leat which fed water from the Barle to the once numerous mills. The last, Town Mills, stopped working in 1971. Silver mining was another local industry but has died a death, unlike the forestry, farming and hunting which continue in the area.

The 12th century tower of All Saints church dominates virtually every view of the town. Looking down over Dulverton from the path alongside, it is not difficult to imagine how the town must have looked in medieval times when the market was open for business in the square fronting the church. Nearby is a former home of the Sydenham family, given to Sir Francis Drake when he married Elizabeth Sydenham. Locate the town hall and you are near the site of the White Hart, a 17th century coaching inn praised in Blackmore's novel 'Lorna Doone' for its 'rare and choice victuals'.

The thought is likely to stir interest in a return to the Bridge Inn or the Lion Hotel again. Cheers!

Lorna Doone

WALK 15: BRUSHFORD

Route: Brushford, Combe Bridge, Nutsford Bridge, Ashill Farm, Combe, Battleton, Dulverton, New Bridge, Brushford

Distance: 5 miles

Map: Ordnance Survey Pathfinder 1256 (SS 82/92)

Start: Brushford church, Pathfinder map reference 919257

How to get there: Brushford is at the southernmost tip of the Exmoor National Park, a mile to the west of the A396 Tiverton to Minehead road, and straddles the B3222.

The Pub

An 'English country sporting hotel' please, if you don't mind: that's the **Carnarvon Arms Hotel** (tel: 0398 23302) near the centre of Brushford

village. And to back up its claim, the privately owned Carnarvon can offer fishing, hunting, riding, shooting, polo, billiards, tennis, golf and squash. That's not to mention the heated outdoor swimming pool. Stabling is available in the grounds, should you wish to bring your own horse or pony (dogs are accommodated there too). And of course we mustn't forget the walking.

If none of those appeals, why not join a safari? Those are laid on too in the form of guided tours of Exmoor using a Land-Rover. As fine a choice of sporting activities as you could wish for.

Or you could simply enjoy the Arms' hospitality.

They pull a fine pint of draught Cotleigh Tawny Bitter by handpump, guest beers too from the keg occasionally. Those are backed up by good food from the popular buttery and even better, certainly better presented, dishes in the dining room. Both bars are comfortable and cosy rather than overwhelming or all enveloping; the diners' being the smaller and more formal of the two. That reflects the 'jackets and ties for dinner, gentlemen please' house rule. No need for that in the garden bar with its patio, which is all the pleasanter for being set in grounds which are a picture. They overlook the Barle river too, where the Hotel has fishing rights. Other than in the garden bar, children are allowed only when having a meal with their parents.

The Carnarvon dates back to 1874 when it was built by the earl himself. At the time it served Dulverton station, which was next door even though the town centre is four miles to the north. The line, part of the Great Western Railway, is long gone. But the station and platform remain, still recognisable and part of the complex of buildings which make up this sporting hotel. You can see the line the trains took too although the track disappeared decades ago.

The Arms, with its three stars from the Automobile Association, has been under the present ownership for more than 30 years. And it shows. Stay a night or nine and enjoy the lounges with their open log fires, antiques, copper and brass galore, richly carved furniture, deep, chintzy armchairs. You cannot overlook either the hunt trophies, the fly cabinets (they have their own stretch of salmon and trout water) and the hunting scenes. The welcome is warm and friendly too, which perhaps is what counts even more. That applies whether you call before or after. . .

The Walk

The sleepy little village of Brushford lies at the southernmost tip of Exmoor and just outside – although only by a few feet – the boundary marking the edge of the national park. It nestles in a fold in the landscape, overlooked by Pixton Hill to the north east, Ash Hill to the north west, and Hulverton Hill to the south. When you are driving northwards, it is easily overlooked: blink as you cross the old Great

Western Railway bridge alongside the Carnarvon Arms Hotel and you will miss it altogether.

Things could so easily have been different. Brushford lies in a seemingly strategic position where the combes and hills rolling down from the north finally level out. Nearby, two of Exmoor's biggest and most important rivers, the Barle and the Exe, meet and combine into one much larger, more powerful waterway. Here, too, there is a major crossroads where the B3223 and the A396, having followed, respectively, the Barle and Exe river valleys, finally join forces in their journey south. Then there was the railway station in GWR days.

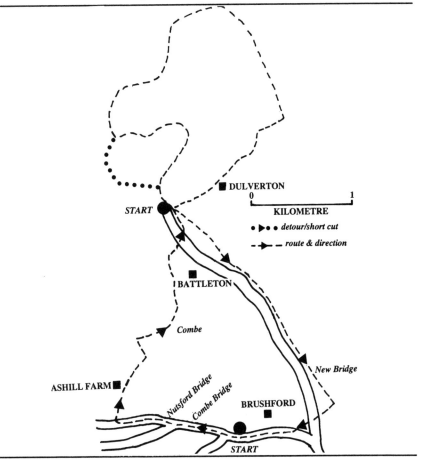

But it was not to be. Perhaps that is just as well. Otherwise our route would not be the pleasant, rural experience it is.

Follow the lane westwards from the church with its stout west tower. If you have time, pause to examine and admire. There is a collection of excellent late Perpendicular windows, some 16th century French stained glass and a rather fine dark Purbeck marble Norman font. Oh yes, and don't miss the effigy of Colonel Aubrey Herbert, also the work of a French craftsman, in the Lutyens-designed north chapel.

Past a second old GWR railway bridge, the lane runs parallel to the River Brockley, a feeder stream to the Exe, as far as Nutsford Bridge where the two swap places. Just to the south was the route of the railway. It it still discernible in places and certainly clearly visible on the map even though 30-odd years have passed since Beeching wielded his line-cutting axe.

The point at which you leave the lane and strike northwards through the fields is marked by a signpost ('Dulverton $1^1/_2'$) and yellow waymark. The footpath may not be clearly defined but the waymarking certainly is; at the right time of year, matching the mass of primroses dotting the landscape. Follow it across the fields, up hill and down dale as the route twists and turns its way around Ash Hill (214m above sea level).

On the gentle descent to the north of Ash Hill, the rolling fields are spread out before you. Leaving a copse to your left, you pass through a farmyard (wellies wouldn't be unwelcome here). Then a gentle climb follows leading to a farm track and so to the crest of another hill.

From here, the hamlet of Battleton, the Barle river valley and Dulverton, nestling among the steeply wooded hills with the moors rising beyond, are spread out before you. The line of the roads and the overall shape of the town are clearly visible. Here you have a suitable spot to pause, catch your breath and survey the scene: it's worth surveying all right.

A brief downhill leg brings you to a lane which shortly joins the B3222. No need to linger: carry on straight across and into Dulverton recreation ground with its trim trail and 1920 war memorial. That leads down to the Barle which you cross courtesy the five-arch medieval road bridge. It runs the magnificent specimen at Landacre, reckoned to be one of the finest in the county, a close second.

The distinctive building with gold weather vane which you leave to your left is Exmoor House, home of the national park authority and a visitor centre where you can top up with maps, books and leaflets.

You soon turn off the main road into Mallam Lane which leaves the town behind and brings you back to the riverbank. It's low-level riverside rambling all the way from here, a delightful contrast with the higher level, hilltop walking earlier.

The highlight of this stretch are the falls and salmon trap you pass just after rejoining the river. The Carnarvon Arms' stretch of water starts just below the falls: watch out for prime specimens of the Greater Protected Fisherman in various types of plumage lurking among the undergrowth. You can tell easily them by their plaintive cry: 'Dammitgotaway'.

Falls on the Barle – watch out for salmon.

Exmoor's boundary runs along this stretch of the Barle. As you follow the course of the river downstream, it is difficult to imagine this placid stream turning into a raging flood. And yet that is what happened during the 1952 Lynmouth flood disaster. This same river uprooted complete trees, tore away the ten-ton stones of Tarr Steps and flooded Simonsbath to a depth of 10ft. Perhaps it was delayed revenge for the damning of the Barle's headwaters to form a seven-acre lake, Pinkery Pond, back in the 18th century. Who knows. . .

Kingfishers are a not uncommon sight on this river. Watch out too for dipper, chiff-chaff, wagtail, stonechat, redstart and heron. A man made focal point along the Barle here is New Bridge, the only river crossing between Brushford and Dulverton. A pretty sight it is too.

Wooded Pixton Hill will by now be looming large to your left. Puzzlecombe Copse, on the far side of the crest and off our route, almost demands investigation. But that will have to wait for another day because the Carnarvon Arms is back in sight. Time for a drink. . .

WALKS 16 & 17: BLACKMOOR GATE

Route 1: Blackmoor Gate, Wistlandpound, Rowley Cross, Rowley Down, Brockenbarrow Farm, Friendship Farm, Wistlandpound, Blackmoor Gate

Route 2: circuit, anti-clockwise, of Wistlandpound Reservoir

Distance: *route 1*, 5 miles; *route 2*, 2 miles

Map: Ordnance Survey Pathfinder 1214 (SS 64/74)

Start: *Route 1:* Old Station House Inn, Pathfinder map reference 646432; *Route 2:* West Park, Pathfinder map reference 638415

How to get there: Blackmoor Gate, Kentisbury, in North Devon, lies on the western edge of Exmoor, approximately half way between Lynton and Barnstaple and straddling the road which links them, the A39, at its junction with the A399 Ilfracombe road.

The Pub

It's called the **Old Station House Inn** (tel: 05983 520) and that's exactly what it is, or used to be: a railway station. That was in the days between 1898 and 1935 when Lynton and Barnstaple were linked by railway, courtesy the L & B line. It ran right through what is now the bar, a narrow gauge 1ft 11^1/$_2$in track spanning 20 miles via nine stations and halts. There is no shortage of photographs and prints on the walls showing the rolling stock and Blackmoor Gate station.

It became an inn in the 1940s. Competition for business must have been brisk at first because of a hotel opposite but that burnt down several years ago. The crossroads here are something of an isolated site because there is no hamlet or village, although it has long been the location of a cattle market.

The Inn itself is a large building which lays well back from the road with plenty of garden and parking space. No shortage of room here to spread yourself in the garden bar when the sun shines: picnic tables and seating galore with plenty more space for the children to tire themselves playing games.

Inside too, under the oak beam ceiling, the T shaped bar stretches on and on. There may only be the one (plus family room) but it divides up naturally enough into 'saloon' and 'public'. In the former, all the fixtures and fittings you would expect. In the latter, a skittles alley, would you believe, as well as the more usual pool tables, darts and what-have-you.

But what about the beer? Real ale in the form of draught Flowers IPA and Flowers Original were on handpump when I called. Guest beers feature occasionally too, including an Exmoor Inns special. That's the name of the company which runs the Inn: they have three other pubs in North Devon.

Snacks and meals are a speciality here and, unusually, include a wide variety of takeaways. The proprietors are particularly proud of their pizzas, baked to order and available with a mouth-watering variety of fillings; and the mussels, locally caught and cooked in four different ways. The *pièce de resistance*, however, must be the home-made sauces, each with its own name. There is, for example, the Peppercorn, with mushrooms, cream, wine and whole green peppercorns; the Provencal, with more than 25 different herbs and spices; and the Cocktail, containing French brandy. Mmmm, delicious!

After all that lot, you will need . . .

The Walks

Route 1:

Straddling as it does the A39, north Devon's main link with the world, Blackmoor Gate has long been viewed as the western gateway to Exmoor. Look at the map and you will see that it neatly plugs a gap between Kentisbury Down (337m) to the west and Rowley Down (365m) to the east.

The boundary of the national park follows the line of the A39 from here to Kentisbury Grange a short distance westwards, then dives off south eastwards shadowing the B3226. It is the same direction that this route follows initially.

After less than half a mile, at Wistlandpound, you strike off north eastwards across the fields. There are few signposts or waymarking and little sign of the footpath on the ground. But you cannot go far wrong because the public right of way follows the southern edge of the hedgerow.

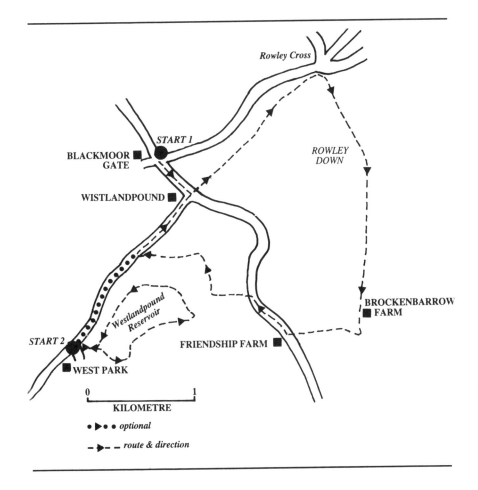

The land rises gently at first, for this is the edge of Rowley Down. But then, after levelling out, you slowly descend briefly to touch the road at Rowley Cross before swinging round clockwise and heading uphill again. Be prepared for plenty of mud if it has recently been wet.

When you reach the highest point, just below the crest of the Down (365m and by Exmoor standards high indeed), pause awhile. The view may not be dramatic but spread out below you across 180 degrees is a broad patchwork quilt of fields, rising and falling, right across the horizon as far as the eye can see. Bootiful.

This walk, like the view, differs from the others on Exmoor. There are no precipitous hills to climb, no steep slopes to descend, no extremes at all in fact, not even any moorland. Just a gentle ramble through pleasant rolling countryside. And very pleasant and enjoyable it is too.

From the highpoint on Rowley Down, head due south, slowly but surely downhill through the fields to reach Brockenbarrow Farm. Follow the lane until Wistlandpound Reservoir comes into clear view below you to the west. Now cut down across the fields, downhill once more to skirt the edge of the coppice of conifers bordering the reservoir before the ground rises to reach the small cluster of buildings which make up Wistlandpound itself.

The final leg leads you up the lane, which just touches the 300m-above-sea-level mark to form a plateau, back to your starting point.

Route 2:

Two options present themselves here. One is to walk up from Wistlandpound to the reservoir entrance and incorporate this short ramble into the first. Unfortunately there is no direct link with the right of way walked earlier. The other is to do it on its own. You choose.

No prizes for guessing that this is a man-made lake, but it is an attractive one at that, with tree-clad banks and fine views over the rolling countryside to the west. Operated by South West Water, the reservoir is fed by numerous springs in the area: look at the Ordnance Survey Pathfinder map and you will notice the surrounding land dotted, in blue, with the symbol 'spr'.

The waters eventually find their way to Barnstaple, becoming in the process the river Yeo which, in turn, feeds the mighty Taw. That disgorges into Bideford Bay 20 miles away as the crow flies to just beyond Barnstaple. Think on that as you circumnavigate the half-mile long lake.

The route, anti-clockwise (but please yourself because the opposite direction is just as pleasant), takes you immediately across the dam. Underfoot, you walk for part of the way on a mixture of man-laid surfaces, hard core, wooden stakes, wire netting. But whether on those, on grass or following the water's edge, the route is always clearly defined and not muddy.

Ahead and up the hill beyond North Thorne is the site of a medieval village. Further round, on the northern bank, you walk along the course of the old Lynton and Barnstaple Railway. There is nothing now to see here of the rolling stock and passengers, other perhaps than the occasional ghost.

The woodland through which you ramble is a mixture. The broadleaf trees are a delight. But the conifers which, fortunately, you can to a large extent avoid, show the unacceptable face of forestry. Between their close-packed trunks, night lasts for 24 hours a day. Nothing stirs and nothing grows.

In contrast, much plant and wildlife and birdlife stirs and grows in abundance elsewhere around, over and in the reservoir. It is a popular bird-watching area and a favourite with fishermen. There is a bird sanctuary here (closed to the public). You will find picnic spots galore and a nature trail. But no refreshments, nor bar. For those, head back to the Old Station House Inn: you will appreciate it now all the more.

WALKS 18 & 19: HEDDON VALLEY

Route 1: Heddon Valley, Invention Wood, Trentishoe Coombe, Black Cleave, Parsonage Wood, Trentishoe Down, North Cleave, East Cleave, Heddon's Mouth Cleave, Birchey Cleave Plantation, Heddon's Mouth Wood, Heddon Valley

Route 2: Heddon Valley, Heddon's Mouth Wood, Heddon's Mouth.

Distance: *route 1,* 4¹/₂ miles; *route 2,* 2 miles.

Map: Ordnance Survey Pathfinder 1214 (SS 64/74)

Start: routes 1 & 2, The Hunter's Inn, Pathfinder map reference 654481

How to get there: the Heddon Valley, in North Devon, lies approximately mid way between Lynton and Ilfracombe in the north western corner of Exmoor. Follow signs from the A39 and A399 and be prepared for steep hills and winding lanes.

The Pub

The Hunter's Inn (tel: 05983 230) may not be easy to reach but once you get there, you will be glad you made the effort. The name conjures up all the right sort of images: an Edwardian country house in a breathtaking setting and all brasses, oak beams and hunting trophies.

Among the memorabilia on the walls are photographs of a large thatched cottage, one of the inn's previous incarnations – there have been several over the centuries, some famed for smuggling. The present building, which replaced one destroyed by fire, is large and rambling.

Among the antlered deers' heads, Victorian candelabra and memorabilia on the walls are photographs of a large thatched cottage, one of the inn's previous incarnations. There have been several over the centuries, some famed for smuggling. The present building, which replaced one destroyed by fire, is large and rambling.

Guests (there are ten rooms) talk of an air of faded Raj. Residents have access to parts other visitors cannot reach. For example there may be only one bar open to walkers in the winter. In addition non residents are restricted to the patio area at the front whereas the landscaped gardens with their streams, statues, ponds and peacocks are a sight to be seen. Being woken by a peacock's call can be more effective than any alarm clock.

Despite all the space, a family room is available only in the summer although children are allowed inside at other times too. Snacks as well as meals are served over the bar throughout the week and there is a restaurant too if you fancy something special.

On the real ale front, the choice varies. Whitbread Flowers Original and Wadworth 6X, served by handpump, are favourites. But you may find Golden Hill Exmoor Ale and Hancocks Cider too along with guest beers in the summer.

The Hunter's Inn – all brasses, oak beams and hunting trophies.

The Walks

Even by the standards of Exmoor, with its hog's-back cliffs and deeply wooded cleaves and combes, the Heddon Valley is an area of extremes. The river may be one of the shorter watercourses draining the moors. However, the valley itself is arguably steeper sided, narrower and more secluded than any other within the national park. But don't be put off because the second of these two walks involves no climbing whatsoever.

As well as being a designated Site of Special Scientific Interest (SSSI) and displaying fine examples of hanging oak woodland, this is National

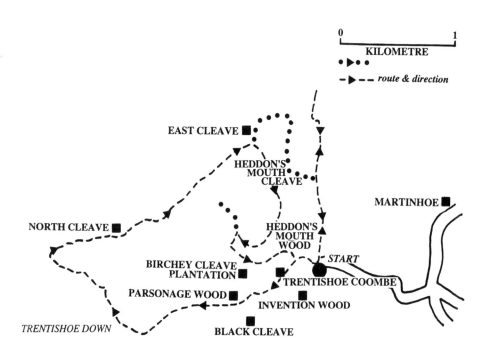

Trust territory. Consequently signposting and waymarking are wide-spread; footpaths, wide and clearly defined. You will find no shortage of them either, with plenty of alternatives and options enabling you to extend, divert or cut short a walk as the fancy takes you.

Route 1

You begin the first route by briefly following the road, known as Jose's Lane, westwards for a few hundred yards before striking south westwards uphill through the oak woodland to your left. The track, Dick's Path, leads you through Invention Wood, still recovering from a storm way back in 1981, to Black Cleave.

Having gained height coming up Dick's Path, you lose it all now to cross a stream which you follow westwards through Parsonage Wood. That links up with a footpath known as Ladies Mile on the edge of Trentishoe Down.

Get ready now for a steep climb over the flank of the Down, which touches 324m at its highest point. Detour to the very top if you wish but be prepared then to be tempted to make another detour to reach the top of the next crest along, Holdstone Hill (348m), which is the highest for miles around.

Nearby are a bevy of Bronze Age barrows and the remains of two Bronze Age huts. The Down itself is a fine example of traditionally grazed coastal heath. It is periodically burnt to rejuvenate the heath. Covered in purple heather, that is a spectacular sight in August.

Without your climbing either crest, the views are panoramic, not least across the Bristol Channel to Wales. You can enjoy them while you regain your breath.

Note the change of waymarking which follows as you head eastwards. Reason: the route now links up with the Somerset & North Devon Coast Path, part of the 515-mile Minehead to Poole South West Peninsula National Trail. Follow that along the clifftop path. But before you do, study the shore-line immediately to the west and see if you can spot the rocky outcrop known as the Mare and Colt.

Below you now is Elwill Bay, at the foot of approximately 150ft-high vertical or undercut cliffs dotted with landslides, or guts as they are known. Don't be tempted down to any of the beaches or coves. It is dangerous here. The only access to the shore is at Heddon's Mouth (where the second walk leads).

Where the route turns inland, a detour is possible, clockwise around the crest of the hill near Peter Rock and down the side of Heddon's Mouth Cleave into the nearly 700ft-deep gorge below.

The main route maintains the high ground, staying just above the steeper slopes, with bird's eye views across the river valley. Tiny Hunter's Inn appears a long way down from this vantage point.

Before beginning the descent into the valley, make a detour to the hamlet of Trentishoe. It was mentioned in the Domesday Book as Trendesholt, meaning spur on the round hill, after the Anglo Saxon word for a circle, 'trendel'. Of most interest is the church, typical of Exmoor and one of the smallest in Devon. Have a look at the minstrels' gallery (about 1731). The hole in the balcony was cut there so that a double bass player's bow could be accommodated. Smugglers apparently used to hide their contraband in the church tower.

Now on the final leg (but hopefully not on your last legs) you head down, down, down into Black Cleave, through Trentishoe Cleave and back along Jose's Lane. At this point, instead of returning to Hunter's Inn you could if you wished carry straight on down to Heddon's Mouth, which is the destination of. . .

Route 2

A shortie, this one. You begin in oak woodland which gradually falls away the closer you get to the sea. The steep, 30-degree slopes to left and right reach for the sky, nearly 700ft-high. Much of the slopes is covered by scree, a frost fragmented jumble of broken rock, here called the Hangman grits. They are so bare because vegetation finds it difficult to gain a hold on the steep and unstable surface.

As you walk, following the course of the not always shallow Heddon river, watch out for a variety of birdlife. Buzzards, pied flycatchers and redstarts are all common. The heron too can be seen here; also the grey wagtail. See if you can spot a dipper, bobbing on the mid-stream rocks or walking along the riverbed, beneath the surface of the water, searching for food. Nearer the shore-line, kittiwakes, fulmars, guillemots and razorbills take over.

And so to the sea at Heddon's Mouth. There are two theories about the name. One says that Heddon comes from the Celtic 'etin', meaning giant. The other, less romantic but more realistic, links the word with the Old English for a heather covered hill. There is certainly plenty of that on the surrounding slopes, so much so that in late summer the colours are almost dazzling in their intensity.

The grey, rocky, shingle-covered beach, although safe in calm weather, should nonetheless be treated with respect. On a stormy day, with a northerly blowing, it can be a majestic and intimidating sight. The view southwards, back up the steeply sided cleave, is an impressive one too. Mouth is a not-inappropriate name for this opening in the otherwise sheer cliff face. And standing guard over the opening, like a huge sentinel, is the dark and forbidding mass of Highveer Point.

Up until 70 years ago, there was a roaring trade carried on over this beach. Limestone and coal, brought by coasters from across the Bristol Channel, were burnt in the kiln just above the high water mark. That was then spread on the fields to reduce the soil's acidity and improve crops. On their return journey the ships carried timber from the coppices of Exmoor for use as pit props in the mines of South Wales.

As you retrace your steps back up the cleave, another detour presents itself, just past the outlet into Heddon river of Hill brook. The path up the steep hillside alongside the brook leads to yet another vantage point on top of the cliffs, Martinhoe Beacon (247m). Here was one of only two Roman (about AD 58) fortlets or signal stations on the whole of Exmoor. And that despite four centuries of Roman occupation. Northwards, beyond the clifftop, look for the rock formation shown on the map as the Cow and Calf.

Now it's back downhill again to the Heddon river and along the foot of the Cleave to Hunter's Inn once more. Hopefully, right on opening time.

WALK 20: SIMONSBATH

Route: Simonsbath, Birchcleave, Flexbarrow, Cow Castle, Two Moors Way, Pickedstones Farm, White Water, Winstitchen Farm, Simonsbath

Distance: about 9 miles

Map: Ordnance Survey Pathfinders 1234 (SS63/73) & 1235 (SS 83/93)

Start: Ashcombe car park, Simonsbath, Pathfinder map reference 774395

How to get there: Simonsbath, in Somerset, is located in the mid west of Exmoor, south east of Lynton. It lies at the junction of the B3358 and B3223, which roads link the A39 with the A396.

The Pub

Exmoor Forest Hotel, says the name on the sign in Simonsbath, appropriately for a pub at the heart of the area known as the Exmoor Forest. By the standards of this national park, Simonsbath (pronounced 'Simmons-bath' please) is, and has long been, a major crossroads. If you wish to cross the moor, as opposed to going around the edges, you will end up passing through the village. It has a pub to match.

But don't get the impression that this is some big, bland, characterless, trunk road drinking house: on the contrary. The Exmoor Forest Hotel (tel: 064 383 341) may be relatively large – there are, after all, 12 bedrooms – but it oozes character and atmosphere, with a friendly welcome to boot. You immediately feel comfortable and at home here.

The single bar itself is not large, at least not at first sight. But the unusual split-level layout plus various nooks and crannies mean that there is more space than you first realise. It keeps things cosy and intimate. On a sunny day, you can take advantage of the garden bar.

Children are catered for. You can get the usual snacks and bar meals or indulge in something more ambitious – local salmon, venison and pheasant for example – in the restaurant if the fancy takes you. Outside the traditional lunchtime and evening licensing hours, morning coffee and cream teas are served.

On draught when I visited were Flowers IPA, Exmoor Ale and Exmoor Stag – those three drawn by handpump; plus Bulmer's Scrumpy, straight from the cask. At certain times of the year you may find guest beers, specials too. Simonsbath Bitter, a house beer by Cotleigh, has been a past favourite.

Whisky (and whiskey) afficionados will have a field day at the Forest. There are 72 labels, malts as well as blended whiskies, from which to choose – the choice used to be more than 300.

In the games room you will find the usual pool and darts plus, dare I mention them, video games. But this being prime huntin', shootin' and fishin' country (there are trophies galore on the bar walls), the landlord can offer a lot more. He has exclusive fishing rights to a 2-mile stretch of the nearby Barle river (brown trout a speciality). Clay and rough shooting can be arranged; also golf as well as coarse and game fishing.

The Barle river – typical Exmoor with trout to prove it.

And of course we mustn't forget something else for which this pub is popular. . .

The Walk

This is one of the Exmoor classics, in the heart of the national park. But despite the words 'Exmoor Forest' appearing all over the map and beautifully sited Simonsbath being described as the forest capital, you should not expect acres of woodland. The name dates back into the mists of time when the area was a forest in the ancient sense of being a royal hunting ground. Forest or no forest, here is Exmoor scenery at its best.

To paraphrase the old song, you take the high road and you take the low road too. Approximately half of this route is along the crest of a ridge; half in the valley bottom. Except that there is virtually no road walking along the way, which makes this pleasant and picturesque walk all the better.

Signposted Landacre (pronounced 'Lannaker') via Cow Castle, the outward leg is nearly all at low level, alongside the Barle river. You start from a free car park in Simonsbath with yellow waymarks pointing the way down to and along the riverbank.

The short leg from car park to footpath passes through a village which was largely the brain-child and creation of the Knight family. John Knight, who came here from Worcestershire in 1819, shaped Exmoor as a whole in a way no other single individual has. Simonsbath was the centre of his 'kingdom'. Here you will pass the school the Knights built and St Luke's church, where the family is buried. But the imprint of their handiwork is evident all over the national park.

The initial descent is through Birchcleave Wood which, despite its name, comprises mainly beech trees. These 115ft-high specimens are more than 150 years old. At 365m above sea level, they are believed to be one of the highest growing beech woods in the country. Time has taken its toll, however, and you will notice large areas where old trees have been felled and a mixture of new ones planted to take their place.

Buzzards can often be seen soaring over the heights of Halscombe and Great Woolcombe to your right. On the river itself you are likely to see

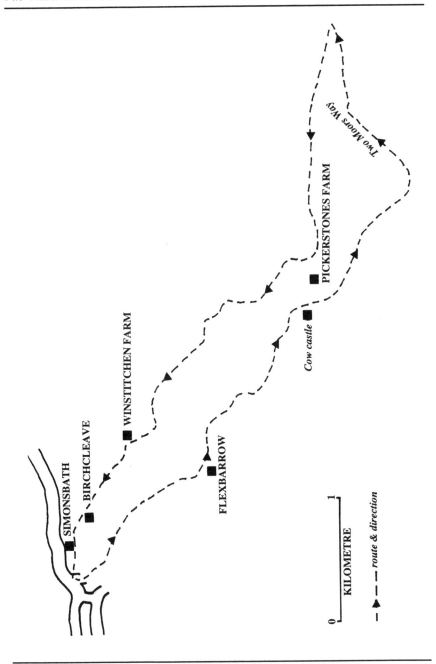

SIMONSBATH

BIRCHCLEAVE

WINSTITCHEN FARM

FLEXBARROW

Cow castle

PICKERSTONES FARM

Two Moors Way

KILOMETRE

0

1

route & direction

herons: they are attracted by the brown trout which are abundant in these waters.

Don't be misled by the placid progress of this river downstream. In 1952 it carried away whole trees, tore down the ten-ton stones of Tarr Steps and flooded Simonsbath to a depth of 10ft. The name Barle means stream from the moors and it was rainwater flowing off those self-same moors which then transformed this stream into a raging flood.

The name of the village is said to come from Simon's Bath, a deep pool in the Barle above the bridge. It was the legendary bathing place of a much-feared local brigand.

Circling inland around the hump of Flexbarrow, the footpath passes the remains of the ill-fated Wheal Eliza, a disused iron ore and copper mine dating back to the mid-1800s. Over the course of 12 years a 300ft shaft was sunk here, mining operations carried on, even a railway started. But all to no avail.

Tragedy came at the end in the form of a 'foul and most unnatural murder' committed by one William Burgess, who killed his young daughter, Anna, and threw her body down the mineshaft. A strange blue flickering light is said to have led police to the body.

A little further downstream is Cow (from the Celtic 'caer' for fort) Castle. There is no mistaking it. This 1,000ft-long Iron Age hill fort holds a commanding defensive position 160ft above the Barle. Climb the mound and judge for yourself: the view says it all. As you admire the outlook from the earth ramparts, which are up to 10ft high, try and imagine the life of the Dumnonii, the tribe who inhabited this area more than 2,000 years ago and from whom the county of Devon took its name.

Nearby a second mound is called, not surprisingly, the Calf. Beyond that you cross White Water courtesy a newly built footbridge. Then you are into a sometimes muddy conifer plantation, still following the course of the river. No prizes for guessing why the hill on the opposite bank is called the Great Ferny Ball.

According to the Ordnance Survey map, a public right of way branches off north eastwards from the eastern end of the plantation. It would provide a short cut back to Simonsbath but there was no sign of the path when I passed this way. So follow the Two Moors Way which stays parallel with the Barle before swinging away uphill.

You leave the river and the valley bottom behind now for the 'high road'. Below, according to the map, is a Hutch. But don't expect any rabbits. This Hutch is a local word for a sluice-gate and marks the point at which Sherdon Water flows into the Barle river. It is a popular spot for swimming.

As you walk up onto the moorland, the fine medieval bridge at Landacre, looking from this height like a child's toy, comes into view. And what a view it is. Three major Exmoor peaks present themselves, all to the south and south east: Brightworthy (428m), Withypool (398m) and Winsford (426m).

A dog-leg left turn at a signpost for 'Simonsbath via Picked Stones' marks the half-way point and a change to red waymarks. This is Braddimore and it's high level walking from here all the way back.

Shortly you come to Picked Stones. It's a quaint name yet simple in its origins. The area, which used to boast a thriving mining industry, is dotted with rocky outcrops. Stones and rocks were cleared by hand in order to improve the ground for growing crops. Hence the name.

Glance down into the valley below for a bird's eye view of Cow Castle. From this angle, the shape of the fortifications becomes dramatically clearer.

Cross the bridge over White Water. This little stream rises only a short distance to the north west near Cloven Rocks bog. There it was that Carver Doone, the robber baron in Blackmore's 'Lorna Doone', was supposed to have been sucked down to his death.

Soon you are walking on ground steeped in yet more history. Here ran one of the most important ancient trackways in Britain, the Harepath. Linking the Midlands with Cornwall, it was used by the Saxons to move men and supplies during their conquest and occupation of Exmoor, around AD 700. The word 'harepath' (or 'herepath') means army road. Nearby on the map is the place name Hereliving.

And so the route leads you back, all the while on the high ground, across the fields and so into Simonsbath again.

Lines of tress and hedgerows forming windbreaks, like this one, are just one sign of the Knight family's activities on Exmoor.

WALK 21: BROMPTON REGIS

Route: Brompton Regis, Lower Rock, Bryant's Bridge, Bryant's Hill, Woolcotts, Wimbleball Lake, Hill Farm, Harewood Farm, Eastern Wood, Wimbleball Dam, South Greenslade Farm, Higher Cowlings, Pulhams Mill, Brompton Regis

Distance: about 5 miles (with the options of a short cut reducing it to 3^1/$_2$ miles and a circuit of the lake increasing it to 13)

Map: Ordnance Survey Pathfinders 1235 (SS 83/93) & 1256 (SS 82/92)

Start: The George, Brompton Regis, Pathfinder map reference 951314

How to get there: located in the south eastern corner of Exmoor (in Somerset), Brompton Regis lies approximately mid-way between Mine-head and Tiverton and about two miles east of the road which links them, the A396. Watch for signs.

The Pub

A traditional village local, that's **The George Inn** (tel: 03987 273) in Brompton Regis. This typical rural pub is located at the heart of this little village, right next door to St Mary's, a typical rural church complete with upstanding 13th century tower. The two buildings are so close that you can study the gravestones in the cemetery when quaffing a pint in the garden bar. Quaint and not at all off-putting. The village, a market town in medieval times, was built around the four sides of the churchyard.

The George nearly didn't make it. When the present landlord took over this free house in the late eighties, it was derelict. No matter what its state then – and it must have been bad – suffice now to say that he has refurbished, redecorated and rejuvenated the Inn. And more power to his elbow. This attractive village, with its cottages dating back to the 16th century, would not have been the same living, breathing, community without it.

Unusually for Exmoor, you will find no hunt trophies decorating the walls of the long single bar. Farming implements down the ages seems to be the theme of the memorabilia spread around the interior. To give you some idea of its length, the bar boasts not just one but two fires; a wood burning stove at one end and an open fire at the other. There are no excuses for not being as cosy as toast on a cold winter's day in this pub.

To keep you even cosier they serve real ale in the form of draught Bass by handpump all year round plus a different guest beer each week in the summer too. Draught Ushers Best Bitter and Taunton Cider, both on handpump, have been favourites in the past.

The usual bar meals are served lunchtime and evenings. Accommodation can be provided should you wish to stay a night or several. There is an area set aside where children are welcome. You will find the ubiquitous darts plus (more's the pity) a juke box and electronic games.

The piece de resistance, however, is a good old fashioned, traditional skittles alley. Voila! The real thing. There's some good fun to be had here.

What else is there to say about The George? Only that the welcome is warm and friendly and the refreshment revitalising. It will set you up for a walk and reinvigorate you afterwards.

The Walk

Part of the pleasure of doing this walk is wandering through Brompton Regis itself. Whether at the beginning or end of the route, which starts and finishes at The George, spend some time sauntering among the buildings.

The royal connection (i.e. the Regis part of the name) dates back a long way, pre-dating even the Norman Invasion. Ghida, the mother of King Harold (he of the arrow in the eye at Hastings), lived, died and was buried here. Both her manor and the Saxon church where she had been buried were razed to the ground after her death.

St Mary's was rebuilt, then rebuilt again in the 15th century and extensively refurbished in the 19th. Inside is a brass, of either 16th or 17th century origin (opinions vary), engraved with a touching poem in memory of a girl of 19. . .

'Reader, Tis worth thy Paines to know
Who was interred here belowe.
Here Lyes good nature, Piettie, Witt,
Though small in volume yet most fairly writ.
She died young, and so oft times Tis seene
The fruit God loves He's pleased to pick it greene.'

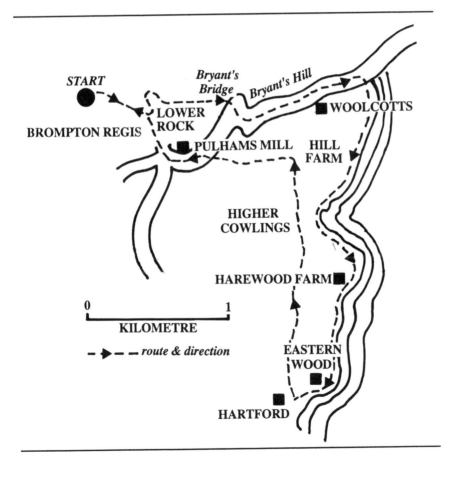

As you leave, just look at that view from the porch of the church. The hills surround Brompton Regis but they are dominated by Haddon Hill (355m) to the south. It is in that direction that our route leads.

There are no signposts nor waymarking to indicate the point at which a public right of way branches off the lane leading out of Brompton Regis to the south east. But you cannot miss it. A footbridge takes you across the swiftly running stream; or you can use the ford if you prefer paddling. This is the Pulham, a tributary of the river which was dammed to make Wimbleball Lake. More of that controversial saga later.

The track is wide, clearly defined – and muddy, so be prepared. As you climb, the views open out around you. At a Y-junction, continue ahead across a stile and keep close to the hedgerow on your right. Notice how the branches have been trained and intertwined horizontally as well as vertically to form an impenetrable structure.

Crossing the fields, you soon descend again – watch for the badger sett to the right. On the skyline ahead, the brown moorland provides a contrast with the green of the fields lower down. A stile gives access through a bank of trees to Bryant's Hill.

Cresting the rise near Woolcotts, you find Wimbleball Lake spread out below you with a swathe of fields on the hillside beyond dotted with pink-washed cottages. The lane leads down to the edge of the lake and a gateway allowing you onto the adjoining land. A signpost points the way: 'dam $1^3/_4$ miles' it says.

This is of course a man-made reservoir, 370 acres in extent, nearly $3^1/_2$ miles long and containing almost 4,500 million gallons of water. It was formed, despite local opposition, by the damming of the River Haddeo in the late 1970s. In the process, part of a deer park, West Hill Wood and a dwelling called Steart were all submerged. But the residents of Taunton, Yeovil and Bridgwater in Somerset together with the good people of Exeter and Tiverton in Devon all see the benefit each time they turn on the tap.

Locals and visitors alike benefit from the leisure opportunities provided by the lake: fly fishing for brown and rainbow trout, dinghy racing, canoeing, rowing, model boat sailing, picnic spots, a nature reserve and of course walks. If you have a dog with you, remember that you and your dog are welcome here, but not in the water: dogs must be kept on leads.

The name Wimbleball? It can probably best be translated as 'pasture among the hills', from the Old English 'winn' meaning a meadow or pasture; and ball, which is a term widely used on Exmoor for a hill. This area is in fact part of the Brendon Hills.

The public right of way along the banks of the lake swings inland to Higher Cowlings just before the sailing club. If required, it provides a short cut back to Brompton Regis which reduces the overall length of this walk by a third. But you miss the most dramatic part of the walk.

The main route continues along the water's edge on a clearly defined footpath which swings around the western side of the sailing club and hugs the lakeside all the way down to the dam. Don't be tempted to cut across the beach alongside the club if launching and retrieving of dinghies is in progress.

The dam, 161ft high, is an impressive and dramatic sight, whether viewed from below or standing on the structure itself. A series of sluices, each like a miniature yet powerful waterfall, keeps the reservoir level constant and maintains the flow of the Haddeo river. Standing at the foot of the dam, you can almost feel the weight of water being held back by the 14 buttresses. There are banks of lights to illuminate the whole edifice at night. It's worth coming back after dark to see the effect.

To complete a circumnavigation of the lake you would at this point cross the dam and continue along the lakeside. A footpath follows or is not far from the water's edge all the way round.

Our route swings northwards up a metalled lane, away from the dam and the Haddeo river, running free now again on its way to link up with the Exe. The lane climbs to a crest, 284m high, with more views across the reservoir to your right, before dropping down once more.

Turn off the lane westwards opposite the entrance to Wimbleball Lake Water Park: a signpost with a yellow waymark points the way across the fields. Be prepared for more mud here. Brompton Regis is now clearly visible ahead, nestling in a fold among the patchwork quilt of fields which covers the hillside.

Over a small footbridge, the final leg of the footpath takes you across two stiles and so onto a lane alongside a house. A short distance further on you pass Pulhams Mill, mentioned in the Domesday Book in 1086. It must have been important.

And so back up the lane into Brompton Regis again, where the George will, as befits the village's name, give you a right royal welcome.

WALK 22: WINSFORD

Route: Winsford, Halse Lane, Winsford Hill, The Punchbowl, Riscombe Combe, Withy Combe, Withycombe Farm, Western Mead Linhay, Ash Lane, Winsford

Distance: about 4 miles (optional detour adds 1 mile)

Map: Ordnance Survey Pathfinder 1235 (SS 83/93)

Start: The Royal Oak, Winsford, Pathfinder map reference 906348

How to get there: Winsford can be found in the south centre of Exmoor. It lies about two miles west of the road linking Minehead with Tiverton, the A396. Watch for signs.

The Pub

The Royal Oak in Winsford (tel: 064 385 455) must be the prettiest pub on Exmoor. That thatched roof with its peacocks, the cream-washed walls, the hanging baskets, the setting next to the village green with its little ford and packhorse bridge: it all adds up to the archetypal rural village inn.

Inside too it's everything you associate with an olde English hostelry. There are the low ceilings, the oak beams, log fires, the inglenook fireplace with a fine iron fireback, the stuffed heads and horse brasses and hunting prints on the wall, pewter tankards hanging from a beam over the bar, Windsor armchairs, big, cushioned, bay window seats. And don't overlook the extensive collection of pottery pet cats. You almost expect it to have featured in one of the great screen classics – perhaps it has. Given its idyllic setting, you could easily understand why.

Most important of all, of course, is the service: what is served and how it is served. There too the Royal Oak comes up trumps. They had two well-kept real ales on draught the last time I was there: Flowers Original

Bitter and Flowers IPA, both on handpump. Draught Taunton cider was also available on handpump – they have had Bulmer's in the past.

The steady bustle and the buzz of conversation plus friendly bar staff all confirm that here is a pub which keeps its customers happy. Children are welcome in the back bar. And don't be surprised to find a horse or two tethered outside while the riders quench their thirst. It's that sort of locality and that sort of hostelry.

There are two bars, lounge and public, in this free house plus table d'hote and à la carte restaurant. That's not to mention the accommodation: eight bedrooms in the main building, which dates back to the 12th century, plus another five in an annex within the courtyard of the inn. In addition, the complex includes a family cottage available for short or long stays. The RAC have awarded the Royal Oak three stars; the English Tourist Board, four crowns.

On a warm, sunny day, it's a pleasure to quaff a drink sitting outside where you can drink in the view too.

The Royal Oak, Winsford – the prettiest pub on Exmoor?

Home-made bar food is served in addition to more elaborate meals. Specialities include filled baked potatoes, smoked fish pate, chicken and leak pies, chopped smoked bacon with button mushrooms and pasta shells in a cream sauce. And various puddings. How about Pineapple Poll, based on an Elizabethan recipe using pineapple puree, green ginger wine and sparkling white wine? Mmmm. Bread is home baked. Menus are changed daily to ensure variety.

In line with the general atmosphere of a rural village inn, there is no juke box, nor any video machines, only the traditional pub games. All in all, it's no wonder the Royal Oak proves popular with visitors, not least those who have enjoyed the countryside at first hand by enjoying . . .

The Walk

Winsford has been described as the prettiest village on Exmoor. So it is worth spending some time simply walking around, drinking up the sights.

With its seven bridges, including an old footbridge and a medieval cobblestone packhorse bridge; its ford and olde worlde English country pub, you can understand why it rates so highly in the popularity stakes. Naturalist and author W. H. Hudson described Winsford in 1909 as 'fragrant, cool, grey green – immemorial peace – second to no English village in beauty, running waters, stone thatched cottages, hoary church-tower.'

That says it all really.

Follow Halse Lane southwards out of the village – it runs right past the Royal Oak. That takes you up across the fields and out onto the edge of Winsford Hill. Where the lane swings sharply south-southwestwards just past a caravan park, our route continues more or less straight on up the hillside.

Look back the way you have come. Below is a panorama patchwork quilt in every shade of green. Ahead, in contrast, the moorland rises before you, a quilt in every shade of brown.

Here you can make a detour, continuing to follow the lane for about half a mile to what is marked on the OS map as an 'Inscribed Stone'. This is

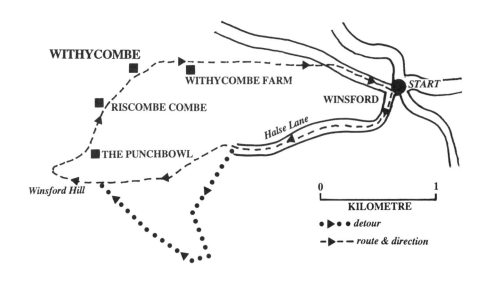

the Caractacus Stone, a relic from the Dark Ages (about 5 – 7 AD or possibly earlier) and one surrounded in mystery.

The stone itself, now enclosed within a stone shelter for protection, stands about 3ft high and is inscribed with the Latin, *Caractaci Nepus*. That translates roughly as kinsman or descendant of Caractacus. He was a courageous Celtic chief whom the Romans took prisoner. There are various legends surrounding the stone, including stories of buried treasure and ghostly horse-drawn carts.

The B3223, which passes close by, will lead you north westwards to rejoin our original route half a mile further uphill than the point where you diverted.

Clearly marked tracks guide the walker to the crest of Winsford Hill, if not the highest point on Exmoor then certainly one offering a unique 360-degree view. This is National Trust property and a popular viewpoint, particularly as it lies so close to the road. From the crest, with

its trig pillar marking a height of 426m above sea level, you can see further than you might imagine. On a clear day even Dartmoor, more than 30 miles to the south as the crow flies, is visible.

Alongside the pillar marking the high point are three fine Bronze Age burial chambers called the Wambarrows. Hard to imagine that they date back between 2,500 and 4,000 years. Truly this area must have been of importance, if not sacred, to our ancestors.

Surrounding you now is high moorland country, open and breezy and covered with gorse, heather, bracken and thorn trees. Here is the haunt of buzzards and wheatears, stonechats and whinchats. This is a favourite feeding ground of the Exmoor pony too. Although larger than the Shetland variety, he still stands only 12 or 13 hands high, with a reddish to dark coat which is impervious to the rigours of a winter spent out here on the moorland.

Head downhill now, following the western rim of the Devil's Punch-bowl. There is the occasional yellow waymark to guide you. Notice the line of trees with their roots standing proud of the ground almost like legs.

It is really only when you have descended almost to the Winn Brook near Withycombe Farm that you will appreciate the full splendour of the Punchbowl. Just pause a while here at its foot. Legend has it that the Devil himself scooped out this hollow with one huge spadeful of rock which he then heaped up to make Dunkery Beacon, the highest point on Exmoor. The bowl is a dramatic and magnificent geological feature, however it came to be formed.

You are now back in among the fields, the bleak and brown, bracken and gorse covered moorland having been left behind. As recently as the late 19th century, the colouring of that moorland would have been more purple than brown. But changing patterns of farming have resulted in a retreat by the heather and an invasion by gorse, or vuzz as it is known. Hence the bleakness of the view above.

A series of yellow waymarks guides you eastwards across the series of fields which follow. These lead you through Withycombe Farm and on to the intriguingly named Western Mead Linhay. In fact a linhay or linney is a local term for an open fronted shed, of the type usually used to house carts, wains or, nowadays, tractors.

Continuing, you cross the fields and eventually come to Ash Lane which you join. You are now in the Exe valley and close by is the Exe river, in the very early stages of its long journey south to the English Channel. It is difficult to associate this shallow stream with the great waterway which disgorges into the sea south of Exeter.

Back on the outskirts of Winsford (pronounced 'Wince-ford' please), you come to the church of St Mary Magdalene, the 90ft tower of which dominates just about every view of the village. In origin it is Norman but there are plenty of signs of later architectural activity, everything from the 12th century to the 20th. Inside, spare a moment to admire the light and lofty interior, the black and white chequered tiling and a Jacobean pulpit.

The best known son of Winsford was Socialist MP Ernest Bevin (1881-1951). Trade union leader, Foreign Secretary in the Labour government of 1945 – 51 and architect of the North Atlantic Treaty Organisation (NATO), he was born in a labourer's cottage in this very village. It is a pretty place indeed, with its bridges and ford, thatched cottages and Norman church. Not to mention the inn of course . . .

WALK 23: UPTON

Route: Lowtrow Cross, Little Moorhouse, Moorhouse Farm, Henstown, Hansetown Road, Venne Cottage, Lyddon's Grounds, Great Moor, Upton Farm, Rainsbury Farm, Hayne Farm, Moorhouse Farm, Lowtrow Cross

Distance: about 6 miles with option of 2-mile extension

Map: Ordnance Survey Pathfinders 1256 (SS 82/92), 1257 (ST 02/12), 1235 (SS 83/93)

Start: Lowtrow Cross Inn, Upton, Pathfinder map reference 017291

How to get there: the Somerset village of Upton is located right on the most south-easterly edge of Exmoor, close to, and south east of, Wimbleball Reservoir. Running through the village is the B3190, which links the A361 (Taunton to Barnstaple road) with the A39 near Watchet.

The Pub

You could easily drive past the **Lowtrow Cross Inn** (tel: 03987 220) without realising it was Upton's pub or that here is a hostelry worth a visit in its own right. It's that sort of place from the outside: unassuming.

It is also some distance from the centre of Upton, to the east, and isolated to an extent, although a glance at the map explains its location. Not for nothing is it called the Cross. This inn lies at what passes almost for a major crossroads in these parts, the meeting place effectively for three roads. Whether you are approaching Upton and points west from north, east or south, you will almost certainly pass this way.

Although it may not appear so, the building itself dates back to the 16th century. The origins of the pub's handle, Lowtrow, which is also the name of the road junction, are shrouded in mystery. One theory links it with France. The other explains it as a derivation of Luttrell, the name of the family which owned Dunster Castle, up in north Somerset, for 600 years.

Originally the inn was a farmhouse. For a period after becoming a hostelry it was unusual in having a Monday to Saturday licence only. The reason apparently is that some of the customers, presumably local farmworkers and possibly in his employ, had one too many and upset the local squire. The result was that a licence for drinking on the Sabbath was withdrawn.

In case you are wondering, a seven day licence is in force now, although it is not unusual for this pub to be closed Tuesday lunchtimes in the winter.

It's a cosy, comfortable place with a warm and friendly welcome where you immediately feel at ease. Unspoilt, rural, village local – those are the terms which come to mind. Certainly it is popular with the locals. Uniquely among the more than two dozen pubs I visited on Exmoor, the Lowtrow Cross boasts its own camping and caravanning site. There is an adjoining cottage too where you can stay.

The oak beamed ceiling is low in the single, spacious bar. That is warmed in the winter by an open fire as well as a wood burning stove. There is an enormous inglenook fireplace. Surprisingly for Exmoor, you won't find any hunt trophies on the walls. The separate games room offers skittles – yes, really – also pool. There is a juke box too and some electronic games (not at all in character with this inn). Children can be accommodated and there are some swings for them outside.

But what about the beer? Well-kept draught Bass and Cotleigh Tawny were on handpump. And you can partake of simple, good value bar food – no frills but plenty for your money. So long as it isn't a winter Tuesday you can enjoy some both before and after . . .

The Walk

High, windy, rolling upland: that's the countryside around Upton. These are the southern foothills of the Brendon Hills, which guard the eastern flank of Exmoor. They form a counterpoint to the Quantocks, the two ranges standing like gargantuan sentries on either side of the Vale of Taunton.

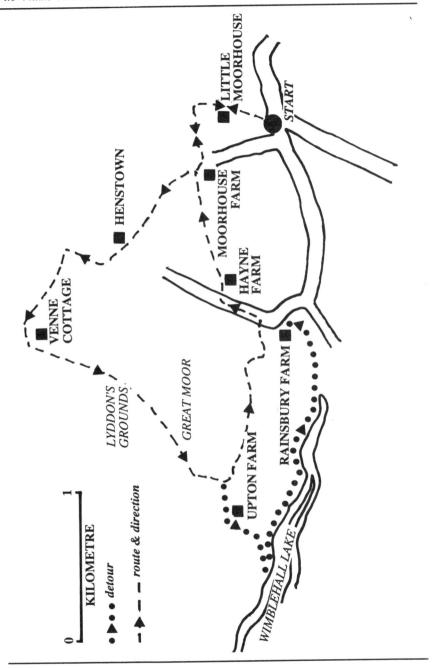

LITTLE MOORHOUSE

START

HENSTOWN

MOORHOUSE FARM

HAYNE FARM

VENNE COTTAGE

LYDDON'S GROUNDS

GREAT MOOR

UPTON FARM

RAINSBURY FARM

WIMBLEHALL LAKE

KILOMETRE

●● detour

▲

— — route & direction

▲

1

0

This is prime farming country. So it comes as no surprise that our walk starts on farmland and navigates its way through no fewer than five farms in total. You pass through the farmyard of only one, however. No surprise either that although several sections are on metalled surfaces, it gets muddy at times, particularly when crossing the fields. But you have no shortage of company en route. There are sheep, lambs (in season), cattle and horses a-plenty.

The start is just to the north east of the Lowtrow Cross Inn – the junction itself is sometimes spelt Lowtree, which is not inappropriate in this neck of the 'woods'. In fact, it's open country here and not wooded at all.

An alternative starting point is further north along the road near Bittescombe Manor which has the advantage of being signposted. Either way, head across the fields, your immediate destination, the cluster of buildings which make up Moorhouse Farm. There is a track running direct to the farm from the B3190 just to the west of the Inn but a public right of way does not connect up with our route, so be sensitive to the farmer's feelings and don't trespass if you can avoid it.

Beyond the farm and maintaining your height, make your way across the fields in a north westerly direction – the route may not be clearly defined on the ground. In the process you cross the fledgling Haddeo river which is the main source of water for the 4,500-gallon Wimbleball Lake just to the south. Hard to believe that it could fill such a large reservoir. It is a mere stream here, not surprisingly really considering that its source lies just a mile to the north, near Cuckold's Combe. Wonder how that got its name . . .

So you come to Henstown, which is barely a hamlet, never mind a town; and Hansetown Road, which barely qualifies for the description 'lane' never mind 'road'. This marks the boundary of the Exmoor National Park and you follow it beyond Venne Cottage to the top of Rugg's Hill. There, a tarmac lane heads gently downhill, initially through a clump of trees. Wimbleball Lake now comes into view over to the west.

This 370-acre, man-made reservoir is the largest stretch of water on Exmoor, which lacks any natural lakes. If you previously had the idea that artificial reservoirs are automatically an eyesore and unattractive intrusions on the landscape, this view of Wimbleball should dispel it once and for all. It could justly be said to complement the surrounding delightfully hilly and wooded countryside. That is despite the fact that a deer park as well as a wood were flooded during the 1970s in the process of constructing the reservoir.

Following a sheep-fold and car park, the lane becomes a track and begins to rise again as it reaches Great Moor. Don't be misled by the name: this is still very much a farming landscape, not moorland. The high point is reached at 313m above sea level, with more views of the lake to match.

On the opposite, southern side of the reservoir is Haddon Hill (355m). See if you can spot any movement. Haddon is home to a herd of Exmoor ponies which the National Park Authority has established in order to support the breed. With his slightly hooded eyes and jutting brow, the Exmoor pony is a dependable, even tempered animal. No wonder visitors fall in love with them.

You descend now, still gently. There are no steep hills or exhausting climbs on this walk. And so you come to Upton Farm. But just before the farm buildings, right in the middle of a field is a church. Or to be more exact, a church tower, seemingly whole and entire yet unattached and complete with cemetery.

This is the original St James', Upton. Since the building of the 161ft-high dam on the opposite bank in the seventies – and you get a good view from this vantage point – part of the original parish has been under water. But that is not the reason for the church's abandonment.

It was originally built in the 14th century to serve the people in the area, then restored in the late 18th. But in 1867 the local bishop decided to build a new church nearer the centre of the village. And so it was, although three bells and the font were removed to the new St James'. A notice inside the tower tells the story: strangely, the address of the writer is given as St Andrew-by-the-Wardrobe . . . The chapel in Upton, incidentally, was built on two levels with a basement stable for the preacher's horse.

Here at Upton Farm you have the opportunity for a detour, which adds about two miles to the overall length of the walk. Take the right of way

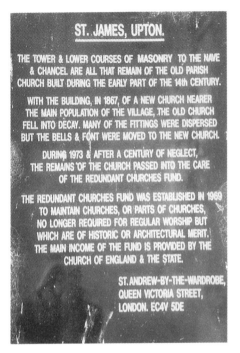

westwards then south west-wards down towards the water's edge. You can then fol-low the line of the reservoir's north bank eastwards back towards the road and Bridge End, rejoining the route just up the lane at Rainsbury Farm.

Otherwise, head eastwards from St James' along a wide, clearly defined farm track to the farm – it rises and falls, twists and turns as it goes but with plea-sant views across the rolling fields. No mud either.

You will find plenty of that on the last leg, eastwards across the fields beyond Hayne Farm, north of the Rectory. It gets particularly marshy underfoot when crossing the infant Had-deo. The footbridge marked on the map was missing when I last passed this way so I used stepping stones. You may be luckier. In any case, it is only a short distance from here to the starting point beyond Moorhouse Farm.

WALK 24: BRIDGETOWN

Route: Bridgetown Wood, Week Lane, Rabbit Wood, Week Wood, Week Bridge, Coppleham, West Howe, Edbrooke Bridge, Week Wood, Bridgetown

Distance: about 3¹/₂ miles plus optional 1-mile extension

Map: Ordnance Survey Pathfinder 1235 (SS 83/93)

Start: Badgers Holt pub, Bridgetown, Pathfinder map reference 924330

How to get there: Bridgetown, in Somerset, lies in the south-eastern sector of Exmoor, right on the A396 and approximately mid way between Dunster (and Minehead) in the north and Tiverton to the south. But don't blink or you will miss it.

The Pub

The Badgers Holt (tel: 064385 204), to the right of the A396 when heading north, is arguably the most conspicuous part of Bridgetown. It might better be renamed Bridgehamlet. Despite the name, this is hardly a bustling centre of population and certainly not a market town. A handful of buildings, post office, pub and that's about it. Not even a full-blown church with tower – for that you have to visit adjoining Exton. Only they don't have the Badgers Holt.

Like Bridgetown itself, 'small is beautiful' would make an appropriate motto for this little hostelry. Also like the rest of the village, it gives the impression of having been shoe-horned into position. A glance at the map shows the reason for the underabundance of space hereabouts: hills, rolling range after rolling range of them.

The main road and a whole string of farms, hamlets and villages are crammed into the river valley here between the hills, the same route as used by the Exe on its journey southwards. Said river valley also has to accommodate a main road, the A396. And as another glance at the map shows, it really is a main road, the only through route from north to south for miles around and the sole A class road through the centre of the Exmoor National Park.

That is without doubt the key to the success and popularity of the Badgers Holt: as well as being a local, it can count on through traffic, passing trade. You will be glad that you didn't, pass by on the other side that is. For this hostelry is a cosy, cheery place.

Sizewise it is larger inside than appears to be the case outside. It has its own car park too. That may be small but there is a layby just across the road so parking should not be a problem, whether to do the walk or visit the pub.

Inside you will find a single bar which, at first and third glance, seems all weathered stone, oak beams and wood panelling. There are the usual hunt trophies decorating the walls, a goodly selection of original paintings by a local artist too. You can buy one if it takes your fancy. An obviously more recently built extension, but one which continues the

The Badger's Holt at Bridgetown.

beams and panelling theme, almost doubles the available space and makes it possible for families with children to be catered for.

Reflecting the type of clientele, there are electronic games, a juke box, a pool table and the ubiquitous dartboard. But this is one Exmoor pub which does not boast a skittle alley. What it can boast is a good drop of real ale, draught Bass and Worthington Best Bitter, both on handpump; hand-pulled Taunton cider too. The usual bar meals are available at lunchtimes and in the evening. Either before the walk, or afterwards or both, you will doubtless find yourself glad of some or all of them.

The Walk

Short and sweet, that's the appropriately tadpole-shaped walk from Bridgetown round West Howe. But while the horizontal distance may be short, there are a couple of steep slopes to negotiate en route. So you walk rather further than appears at first sight and get some good, chest expanding exercise into the bargain.

A signpost marked 'Coppleham $1/_2$ mile' points the way, northwards from Bridgetown along the banks of the infant Exe river. Two points of interest to bear in mind as you pass through this hamlet, in the parish of Exton. It may not be able to compete with its Caribbean namesake in Barbados. And it may not have a church with a tower. But it does, or rather did, have a chapel, albeit now concealed within the dwelling place to which it was adapted. In addition, this little community can boast their very own cricket ground. So there.

You soon leave the road, bisecting the waterway using the crossing which gave Bridgetown its name. There isn't a comparable crossing to the south until you reach the main turning for Dulverton, a good six or seven miles away.

This is hunting country, the haunt of the Devon & Somerset Staghounds. Just to prove it, the hunt was out in force the last time I walked this route. As I made my way upstream, a red deer with a full set of antlers appeared on the hillside above, raced across the fields and disappeared into a copse above Edbrooke Wood. I never did discover its fate. But it proved that keeping one's eyes peeled for a sight of this majestic animal in the area need not be a fruitless exercise.

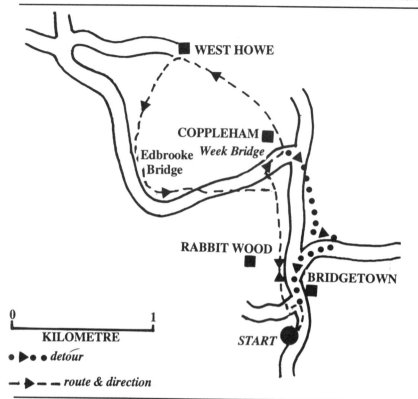

WEST HOWE

COPPLEHAM

Week Bridge

Edbrooke
Bridge

RABBIT WOOD

BRIDGETOWN

0   1

KILOMETRE

● ▶● ● *detour*

— ▶ — — *route & direction*

START

Although initially you pass through what looks suspiciously like a scrap metal yard, the riverside footpath is thereafter wide, clearly defined and typically Exmoor in its setting. Birdlife abounds both in the meadows and woodland. Watch in particular for herons near the weir and pheasants everywhere.

That brings us back to hunting again because this area is a breeding ground for game birds. Witness the 'beware pheasants for six miles' roadside signs. Heaven knows how many get run over but going on my observations the count must run into treble figures on occasion. Don't be tempted to snaffle a brace for dinner. . .

At Coppleham a sign confirms that you are in the midst of a game reserve. Another gives you a choice. Howetown, it says; $1^1/_4$ miles by bridleway or half a mile by footpath; the low road or the high road. Our route takes the high road short cut, over the top of West Howe hill rather than around it – that comes later.

Confirmation that you are on the right track will come from the sight of a large, a very large, dovecot near a small cluster of houses. Then it's up, up, up the hill, leaving Coppleham, its houses and its Week Bridge all behind and below.

After passing through a gateway, the first of many as you cross this hill, the path forks: take the rising left hand branch heading north-northwest. The public right of way follows a hedgerow, which you keep on your right hand side as you pass from field to field, rising steadily.

The crest of West Howe hill tops 289m. But our route passes to the north of the very top, maintaining a straight line. Or as straight a course as it is possible to maintain when walking across country and over a hill.

The climb might have involved some effort but the resulting panorama makes it all worthwhile. From your vantage point near West Howe Barn you have a clear view along not just one but two river valleys. To the north is the Quarme, striking due south from its source on Codsend Moors near Dunkery Beacon. To the north west, and circling around two sides of the hill on which you are standing, is the Exe, one of Exmoor's most important and impressive waterways. Their meeting place is close by the weir passed earlier.

Below you to the north west, Winsford, Exmoor's prettiest village, is displayed in all its glory. From this height it looks like a model village. Due west is the mass of Winsford Hill (426m). At the foot of West Howe hill, almost at your feet it seems, is West Howetown, like Bridgetown another hamlet with big ideas about its position in life.

Time to descend. Near the foot of West Howe hill you pick up a bridleway, the one signposted earlier from Coppleham. Follow it in an anti-clockwise direction and after passing through some woodland, the waymarked and signposted route brings you back to the banks of the Exe.

Don't be tempted to cross the river at Edbrooke Bridge: it is private. Continue on along the north bank of the river until you come to a newly built and rather novel footbridge. Why novel? Just look at the counterbalancing arrangement which makes up the 'gateway'. Clever stuff.

You are now on Edbrooke Road but to avoid continuing along the highway, take the track which bears right, south eastwards, and leads up into Week Wood. That cuts the corner where Edbrooke Road joins the A396 and returns you to the initial leg of the walk, the tadpole's tail.

And so back to Bridgetown. But, if you have time, not before paying a visit to Exton's church (complete with tower). A bridlepath will take you there if you cross the A396 at Coppleham Cross.

The building is worth the detour, clinging as it does to the steep hillside on the outskirts of the village. That tower is castellated and no less than 700 years old. Outside, there are fine views westwards across the wooded valley. Inside, look for the handsomely lettered panel dedicated to Rose Pierce (about 1712) with its macabre trappings: a crowned skeleton, Old Father Time and a skull-and-cross-bones. Broad Lane leads you back downhill and directly into Bridgetown just north of the Badgers Holt.

WALK 25: LUXBOROUGH

Route: Monkham Wood, Perley Combe, Withycombe Common, Rodhuish Common, Monkslade Common, Slowley Farm, Stout's Way Lane

Distance: 4 miles

Map: Ordnance Survey Pathfinder 1235 (SS 83/93)

Start: Monkham Wood Forestry Commission Depot, Pathfinder map reference 985379

How to get there: Luxborough is located in the middle east of Exmoor, tucked well away from main roads. From either the A396 or A358, take the B3224 then watch out for a road sign pointing northwards down a narrow country lane.

The Pub

I have saved the best till last. **The Royal Oak** (yes, another, except that this one is also known as the Blazing Stump) is a real gem (tel: 0984 40319). It is said to date back to the 14th century although the present building is more 18th century. Either way, here you have a watering hole worth making a detour to visit. Genuine, completely unmodernised, real olde worlde flavour. All flagstones, log fires, cobblestones and scrubbed wood furniture. Plus the best choice in real ale of any of the more than two dozen pubs sampled on Exmoor.

When I visited, you could choose from three regulars, Flowers IPA, Cotleigh Tawny Bitter and Exmoor Gold. Only the Flowers was on hand pump, all the rest being straight from the barrel. But in addition there were four guest beers, Batemans Champion Premium, Abbot Ale, Courage Directors and Beamish Irish Stout. Up to five, including cider, are stocked during the summer. The more than 100 beer mats pinned to the oak beams above the heads of the drinkers tell the tale. As the friendly and talkative landlord, Robin Stamp, was quick to point out, they are virtually all 'genuine'; that is, brews served, either now or in the past, over the bar here.

There are two. of those, plus a snug and an additional, family, room which, unlike the rest, has scrubbed floorboards rather than flagstones. Two large, open log fires keep things cosy in the winter. And no piped music or electronic games whatsoever.

Food is cooked to order so it should satisfy. Full meals as well as snacks and sandwiches, all served from the bar, are on offer at lunchtimes and in the evening. For a treat, sample the home-made port and Stilton pate. Children and vegetarians are catered for too. And there is a garden bar for sunny, summer's days. No wonder the Royal Oak was voted CAMRA's top pub in the South West for 1991.

The Walk

To go with this gem of a pub, a jewel of a walk with a few surprises along the way just waiting to be sprung.

A depot doesn't sound like the most auspicious of starting points but the Forestry Authority's office (more of a hut really) at the entrance to Monkham Wood is small, unobtrusive and quickly left behind. You head uphill, leaving the tarmac behind for a track which is wide and stony, a signpost pointing the way to Dunster with a blue waymark confirming the route. To the left, views across Perley Combe; to the right, the wood.

Within the space of the mile-long climb it changes character markedly. At times the trees are mixed, deciduous and coniferous, large and small, of all shapes, sizes and colours. Then the mix changes, with Christmas trees predominating but still a good sprinkling along the fringe of broadleaf specimens. For part of the way, however, there is nothing but tightly packed evergreens, the interior as dark as night, silent, almost sinister. Certainly a forest of conifers is not the most welcoming of environments.

But our clearly defined route, with its blue waymarks, passes straight through and the contrast between the gloomy evergreens and the open space which follows makes the latter all the more enjoyable.

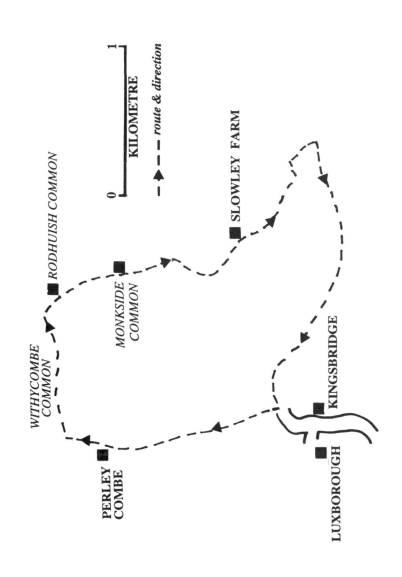

This is Withycombe Common and now you come to a crossroads. It's like the hub of a wheel, with the spokes comprising seven footpaths. The signpost here, which reveals that the track you have just walked is Bellas Lane, gives destinations for all except the one we take. Head north-northeast.

You will soon know you have made the right choice.

As the track climbs gently, the land around you drops away until by the time you reach the trig point, 381m, you can see (how did the song put it?) almost forever. Your first surprise is the seagull's-eye-view of Minehead, to the north. Then you realise that, beyond, the Welsh coast is visible too. The biggest surprise is when you turn eastwards and see the Doniford river valley spread out before you with the Quantocks marking the horizon. Down on the coast is Watchet; inland, Williton. Well to the south east is Bishops Lydeard – is that Taunton just visible beyond? If you are lucky, you might even catch a glimpse and the sound of the West Somerset Light Railway, which follows the course of the Doniford.

Having drunk your fill of the panorama from that viewpoint continue, downhill, drinking in even more of the sights as you go. Ahead now, across Bridgwater Bay and the Bristol Channel, stretches the length of the Severn Estuary. Spot the bridge if you can. More likely to be visible are the stubby islands of Steep Holme and Flat Holme with, beyond them, Cardiff.

Taking the track heading south east, you skirt Rodhuish and Monkslade Commons. To your right, beyond a swathe of felled trees looking like something from the Somme, lies another thick and gloomy bank of conifers. But to your left are continuing views across the valley to the Quantocks. This track is like a gallery with a patchwork quilt spread out for your delectation below you: a vista of fields of every shade of red (the sandstone soil) and green intersected by hedgerows and punctuated by clumps off trees with little clusters of farm buildings and hamlets here and there.

A signpost directs you on towards Slowley Farm. Crossing a field followed by a stretch of heath covered in gorse, you then begin your final descent. The path on the ground may not be clear at this point but simply head south east, skirting the bank of trees to the south and, if all

View on the final leg: Stout's Way Lane.

else fails, following the fence on the edge of the bank until some farm buildings appear ahead. This is Slowley Farm which brings you to Stout's Way Lane.

Make your way as quickly as you wish past Slowley Wood, where there are more signs of devastation to the trees. Whether caused by the Forestry Authority or natural forces wasn't clear. The lane wends its way steadily downhill, with a fairly steep drop on your left down to the Washford river via the intriguingly named Druid's Combe Wood. More brooding conifer plantations. More Christmas trees. And then you are back at the starting point again. A fitting finale.

Explore the countryside with Sigma!. We have a wide selection of guides to individual towns from Buxton to Lancaster, plus outdoor activities centred on walking and cycling in the great outdoors throughout England and Wales. Here are some recent highlights:

PEAK DISTRICT DIARY - Roger Redfern
An evocative book, celebrating the glorious countryside of the Peak District. The book is based on Roger's popular column in *The Guardian* newspaper and is profusely illustrated with stunning photographs. *£6.95*

I REMAIN, YOUR SON JACK - J. C. Morten (edited by Sheila Morten)
A collection of almost 200 letters, as featured on BBC TV, telling the moving story of a young soldier in the First World War. Profusely illustrated with contemporary photographs. *£8.95*

There are many books for outdoor people in our catalogue, including:

HERITAGE WALKS IN THE PEAK DISTRICT
- Clive Price

EAST CHESHIRE WALKS
- Graham Beech

WEST CHESHIRE WALKS
- Jen Darling

WEST PENNINE WALKS
- Mike Cresswell

NEWARK AND SHERWOOD RAMBLES
- Malcolm McKenzie

RAMBLES AROUND MANCHESTER
- Mike Cresswell

WESTERN LAKELAND RAMBLES
- Gordon Brown

WELSH WALKS: Dolgellau and the Cambrian Coast
- Laurence Main and Morag Perrott

WELSH WALKS: Aberystwyth and District
- Laurence Main and Morag Perrott

Cycling in The Cotswolds
– Stephen Hill

OFF-BEAT CYCLING IN THE PEAK DISTRICT
- Clive Smith